John Oliver
Corporate Trauma

John Oliver

Corporate Trauma

The toxic legacy of a crisis

DE GRUYTER

ISBN 978-3-11-157083-9
e-ISBN (PDF) 978-3-11-157112-6
e-ISBN (EPUB) 978-3-11-157129-4

Library of Congress Control Number: 2025943142

Bibliographic information published by the Deutsche Nationalbibliothek
The Deutsche Nationalbibliothek lists this publication in the Deutsche Nationalbibliografie;
detailed bibliographic data are available on the internet at http://dnb.dnb.de.

© 2025 Walter de Gruyter GmbH, Berlin/Boston, Genthiner Straße 13, 10785 Berlin
Cover design: Ion Jonas, Berlin
Typesetting: Integra Software Services Pvt. Ltd.

www.degruyter.com
Questions about General Product Safety Regulation:
productsafety@degruyterbrill.com

If at first the idea is not absurd, then there is no hope for it
Albert Einstein

Praise for Corporate Trauma

"Serial failed corporate turnaround . . . there's a strong case for the idea of Corporate PTSD"
　　Chris Brady, Chief Intelligence Officer, Sportsology

"Corporate Trauma offers important lessons for any leader seeking to implement transformational change"
　　Satyen Dayal, Managing Director, Edelman (UK)

"An original examination on how crises can cripple corporate innovation and agility"
　　Juliet Ecclestone, Platform Economy U.K. Chair

"A novel analysis on how a company's past can hinder its future"
　　Amanda Evans, Media Consultant & Journalist

"A groundbreaking explanation of why new CEOs keep failing to turnaround firms"
　　Richard Fogg, CEO, CC Group

"An interesting take on the persistence of failure in complex organizations"
　　James Gater, Director, Special Project Partners Ltd.

"It is rare to come across a business book that is genuinely innovative"
　　Emmanuel Gobillot, Strategy Consultant

"An innovative perspective on how organizations can be held captive by their culture"
　　Lucy Kung, Strategic Adviser & Senior Research Associate, Oxford University

"A book that explains why your company's past could be holding back its future"
　　Maria Santacaterina, Global CEO and Consultant

https://doi.org/10.1515/9783111571126-202

Imagine . . .

a business suddenly struck by a devastating event – a cyberattack, a natural disaster, a major lawsuit. The initial impact is shock and disbelief. In the aftermath, the business experiences unpredictable fluctuations in performance and psychological symptoms like low employee morale, recurring flashbacks to the crisis, strained relationships and an erosion of stakeholder trust. There are even physical symptoms like a plummeting share price, declining revenue, rising costs and mounting debt. While these challenges are understandable, some businesses struggle to recover normal operations and return to profitability. They may become paralyzed by fear, unable to adapt to a changing competitive landscape, and ultimately succumb to the lingering effects of the crisis. They are suffering from a collective trauma . . . Corporate Trauma!

https://doi.org/10.1515/9783111571126-203

Preface

The journey of an idea . . .

Park Avenue, Manhattan, New York – May 2016. I'm meeting with Martin Reeves, Senior Partner and Chairman of the BCG Henderson Institute, the Boston Consulting Group's 'think tank' dedicated to developing innovative new insights for business and management practice. With a highly successful career in management consulting, an MBA and MA in Natural Sciences, and a recent publication in the Harvard Business Review on *The Biology of Corporate Survival*[1], Martin was the obvious candidate to consider an unconventional idea at the intersection of biology and business.

Martin had responded favorably to my email 'pitch' a month earlier and had cleared time in his busy diary to meet and discuss an idea that drew on insights from the biological field of Epigenetics to better understand the impact of corporate crisis events on organizational culture and performance. Needless to say, Martin provided me with detailed and critical feedback which shaped the development of *Corporate Trauma* as a concept.

103rd Street on the Upper West Side of Manhattan, New York – May 2016. I met with Robert M. Randall, Editor of Strategy & Leadership. My article submission on Corporate Trauma had been unequivocally rejected by two reviewers as 'nonsense', and yet, Robert had found the idea both intriguing and highly innovative. Over lunch, we discussed the concept further and he advised me that he was going to publish the article in a 2017 issue.

The idea of *Corporate Trauma* starts to become more robust during my Visiting Fellowship at Green Templeton College, University of Oxford in 2016. The serendipitous merger of Green College (medical studies) and Templeton College (management studies) in 2008 had provided me with an ideal environment in which to study an idea that challenged the conventional wisdom that corporate performance is largely determined by organizational strategies and market conditions. The notion of *Corporate Trauma* offered a new lens through which to understand the long-term consequences of a crisis on a company's culture and financial performance, even after the immediate threat had passed.

10, Hudson Yards on Manhattan's West Side, New York – April 2018. Described as the office of the future by Fortune magazine, I was back to see Martin Reeves at the Boston Consulting Group's swanky new office with 360-degree views of New York's skyline. The meeting focused on the 'metrics' that would pro-

---

1 Reeves, M., Levin, S., & Ueda, D. (2016). The biology of corporate survival: natural ecosystems hold surprising lessons for business. *Harvard Business Review*, 94(1–2), 47–55.

https://doi.org/10.1515/9783111571126-204

vide evidence of chronic corporate underperformance and serial failed turn-around attempts. The usual suspects of a comparative analysis of Market Capitalization, Earnings Before Interest and Taxes, and Operating Income were briefly discussed. However, levels of firm innovation and vitality added an intriguing new dynamic to the conversation.

An idea once considered 'nonsense' was now gaining traction, and in 2018, the British Academy funded my research following a highly competitive process. Entitled 'Investigating the culture of chronically underperforming firms: past, present and future' the grant enabled me to develop a conceptual framework and robust methodological process to identify *Corporate Trauma* in organizations.

Edelman (UK), London – December 2019. It was time to road test the idea of *Corporate Trauma* with practitioners. Satyen Dayal, Managing Director, arranged for me to present the concept to their highly experienced Crisis and Reputation Risk Team. The feedback was positive and the participants were fully engaged in what can only be described as a 'left-field idea' that could have potential as a valuable framework for communications consultants by providing a new lens through which to analyze corporate crises. It could also provide management consultants with a better understanding of chronic corporate underperformance and serial failed turnarounds. However, more cases studies would be needed to further embed the idea that a corporate crisis could create long-term and chronic effects in an organization. These would be presented in a few months' time. However, by March 2020, a global crisis in the form of the COVID-19 pandemic had put paid to a follow-on workshop and my theoretical idea on how a crisis could create a lasting trauma in an organization had been overtaken by a once in a 100-year real life crisis.

Nevertheless, the global pandemic provided me with a unique opportunity to submit evidence to the Business, Energy and Industrial Strategy Select Committee inquiry on *The impact of coronavirus on businesses and workers*. My testimony and publications on *Corporate Trauma* were cited and published by the committee in their interim pre-Budget report on 26th February 2021[2]. The evidence argued that crises like COVID-19 could have a severe and lasting impact on business performance and workforce productivity, affecting organizations for years, not merely in the short term. Consequently, a coherent strategic approach was essential for government and policymakers to navigate both the immediate challenges

---

2 House of Commons, Business, Energy and Industrial Strategy Committee. The impact of Coronavirus on businesses and workers: interim pre-Budget report Second Report of Session 2019–21. Published on 26th February 2021.

and the protracted "transgenerational effects" and adaptive responses that could adversely affect business performance.

In 2021, I also had an online meeting with a senior executive from the Investor Relations team of a company featured in the book's case studies. He expressed surprise and shock upon seeing my presentation on how the company's approach to innovation and risk had changed in the aftermath of a significant crisis that the company had endured years earlier. His initial reaction was defensive, questioning the origin of the data. He was clearly taken aback when I informed him that the information was sourced from the company's annual reports. He also noted that my presentation effectively conveyed the shock and hidden trauma that the company had experienced. At this point, I knew that I was really on to something!

Confederation of British Industry, London – September 2023. I presented *Corporate Trauma* to a group of senior executives at a knowledge exchange event. Delegates from aerospace, defense, management consulting, strategic communications, journalism, governance and policy found the idea thought-provoking, and like many delegates from other business and academic conferences that I have presented to over the years, they used a common phrase . . . "why didn't I think of that".

It has been a long and interesting journey. However, the next part of the journey will depend on you, the reader. Will you embrace an unconventional idea, put the concepts presented in this book into practice, and make a positive impact on your business? My advice is to, firstly, identify the key takeaways that resonate with your specific challenges or goals. Second, look for opportunities to apply these ideas in your daily work, whether through small experiments or significant strategic shifts. Third, network with like-minded individuals to discuss the book's impact and share experiences. By actively participating in this process, readers can transform the idea of *Corporate Trauma* into actionable knowledge that produces tangible results.

I hope that you find the book, in the words of Albert Einstein, an absurd idea that could just be plausible!

Contents

Chapter 1
The Turnaround Playbook Reimagined

Albert Einstein reputedly said, *'if at first the idea is not absurd, then there is no hope for it'*. The implication being that truly groundbreaking and innovative ideas often seem unconventional, and that the more outlandish or counterintuitive they seem, the greater the potential for them to be truly transformative. Furthermore, ideas that are immediately understood or accepted are likely to be incremental improvements on existing knowledge or practice, rather than revolutionary breakthroughs. The most imaginative and impactful ideas, therefore, often challenge our existing understanding of the world and require a 'leap of imagination' that takes you beyond the ordinary, or expected, and by connecting seemingly unrelated concepts, something entirely new is created.

This book broadly addresses the issue of chronic corporate underperformance and serial failed corporate turnaround attempts. The conventional approach used by executive boards and management consultants is to treat every problematic corporate rehabilitation as a routine turnaround case. The 'classic turnaround playbook' is equally conventional; appoint a new Chief Executive Officer (CEO) and leadership team whose primary purpose is to take swift action to rescue the staggering firm from potential failure. Their initial goal is to restore profitability, primarily by financial restructuring to manage debt, aggressively managing costs, and operational overhauls to improve efficiency. When survival of the firm is in sight, they can start refocusing the business on areas of future growth potential. While specifics may vary depending on the industry and the unique circumstances of the distressed company, the core components of this playbook are remarkably consistent.

There are many examples from diverse sectors like technology (Kodak, Nokia, Yahoo), retail (American Apparel, Boohoo, JCPenney, Ted Baker, The Body Shop, RadioShack), entertainment (Blockbuster, Flud, Quibi, Vine) and automotive (Chrysler, General Motors) which highlight the dangers of failing to recognize the threat posed by new market entrants, and or, being unable to adapt to changing consumer preferences, technological advancements or economic trends. In each case, multiple attempts to revitalize a struggling company through drastic meas-

https://doi.org/10.1515/9783111571126-001

ures such as restructuring, cost-cutting, market re-positioning, and expediently launching new products and services have ultimately failed to turnaround the fortunes of these firms. A common reason for serial failed turnarounds is a lack of strategic clarity with companies pursuing multiple, often conflicting strategies, leading to confusion and inefficiencies. Another pitfall is a failure to address the 'underlying' cultural issues that might have contributed to the decline in the first place. A toxic work environment, lack of employee engagement, or resistance to change can also hinder turnaround efforts. Furthermore, an inability to adapt to external pressures in the form of economic downturns, increased competition, or regulatory changes can create additional and often insurmountable challenges for an organization already in decline.

Disorientated, confused and lost in a maze of endless corridors and dead ends, each new turnaround strategy is a path taken and a promise of escape from the corporate wilderness. Yet, every turn leads to another dead end, another failed attempt to find the exit. The company is lost and trapped in a cycle of false starts, misguided efforts and chronic underperformance. As the walls of the maze close in, the once-promising corporate reset of every newly appointed CEO soon becomes yet another desperate fight for survival. The longer the company remains lost, the feeling of being trapped grows and the uncertainty of finding the way out leads to a downward spiral of stress and anxiety. Perhaps there is another way out of the maze?

The Hidden Killer of Corporate Turnaround

This book raises an important question. What is the playbook for a company who has appointed numerous new CEOs to turnaround the organization, but ultimately failed? This is where Albert Einstein's famous quote comes back into play. It's time to consider an unconventional idea that requires the reader to think outside the box and take a mental jump to a new world that challenges existing assumptions on how serial failed turnarounds are evaluated. It's time to consider an innovative new concept . . . Corporate Trauma.

Corporate Trauma argues that there could be a 'hidden killer' of corporate turnarounds that hampers successive CEOs attempts to revitalize an organization. The central thesis of Corporate Trauma asserts that organizations with a history of persistent failure and unsuccessful turnaround attempts could be suffering from a *'stress reaction'* to a previous crisis event that continues to inhibit its ability to successfully address new market challenges. This book argues that when such situations can't be resolved by a change in strategy, or a new CEO, it is time to consider a thought-provoking *'alternative diagnosis'* that has the potential to make a transformative impact on the way prolonged corporate underachievement and serial failed turnarounds are evaluated and managed. That alternative has been inspired by *Epigenetics.*

Epigenetics, a relatively new field in biology, studies how environmental factors like diet, stress, famine, and toxins can change gene expression (how genes are turned on or off) without altering the DNA itself. Numerous studies have shown how these changes can contribute to diseases like cancer, diabetes, and mental health disorders. Importantly, these changes are 'inherited' by multiple generations following the initial exposure which is referred to as a *'transgenerational response'.*

The idea of Corporate Trauma builds an intellectual bridge and transfer of knowledge between discrete fields of study (business and biology) in order to gain new insights which could help to better understand the problem of chronic corporate underperformance and serial failed turnarounds. It argues that prolonged corporate decline and stagnation may not always be attributed to the current leadership or strategic decisions, but rather to the lingering effects of a past crisis. Indeed, a corporate crisis can create dysfunctional adaptive attitudes and behaviors that subsequently become embedded in the culture of a firm to the detriment of its long-term viability and performance. By applying Epigenetic concepts, this book argues that the trauma of a significant event, such as a financial crisis or major scandal, can leave lasting scars on an organization's culture, employees and performance. Importantly, the epigenetic markers of an organization suffering from trauma, often hidden and overlooked, are 'inherited' from one generation of a firm to another, which in turn, hinders subsequent turnaround attempts. By recognizing the potential impact of transgenerational responses following a corporate crisis, leaders and consultants can better diagnose the hidden causes of Corporate Trauma and develop more effective turnaround strategies. Instead of treating each organization as a 'routine turnaround case' they should consider each turnaround in the context of the organization's history and address the underlying issues that may be hindering its health and development.

Purpose, Value And Structure Of The Book

The purpose of this book is to offer a new lens through which to analyze cases of chronic corporate underperformance, and in particular, those organizations with a history of serial failed turnaround attempts. The central tenants of Epigenetics thinking have been used in this book to argue that organizations suffering from persistent strategic drift and underperformance could be suffering a *'stress reac-*

tion' to a previous corporate crisis that has produced a *'hidden trauma'* which is *'inherited'* by successive CEOs attempting to turnaround the firm.

In essence, this book provides a valuable diagnostic tool for understanding the short-term effects and long-term consequences of a corporate crisis. It reveals how such crises can create hidden shifts in company culture that negatively impact performance. Business leaders, managers, and consultants can use this tool to better understand an organization's dynamics. By examining a significant event in the organization's history, the book shows how to identify and manage the resulting dysfunctional responses, and adaptive negative attitudes and behaviors that have become ingrained in the culture of the organization which subsequently hinders performance. This understanding is crucial for navigating change and developing effective solutions to improve performance. As such, there are a number of areas where an understanding of *Corporate Trauma* can play a crucial role in an organizations performance and development. These include:

Corporate Turnaround: when a struggling business can't improve its finances, operations, or competitiveness, *Corporate Trauma* suggests an innovative new approach. Instead of just looking at the numbers and processes, the book urges leaders and consultants to consider whether a past crisis has left a lasting trauma. It argues that repeated failed turnarounds might stem from this trauma, and that successful turnarounds must address the ingrained, negative attitudes and behaviors that developed as a result of the past crisis.

Crisis Management and Strategic Communication: organizations facing a crisis activate their crisis management plan to limit damage and restore normal operations. Crucially, they must communicate effectively with stakeholders, providing timely, accurate, and transparent information to manage perceptions and prevent rumors. While a post-crisis recovery plan focuses on rebuilding reputation, the book urges communications consultants to consider the potential traumatic and long-term impact of a crisis on the organization and its ability to fully recover.

Corporate Brand Management: the long-term impact of a crisis on the corporate brand reputation can be substantial and multifaceted. A tarnished reputation can make it challenging to recruit and retain skilled employees, which in turn, can impact levels of innovation and long-term growth. The book argues that a crisis can create a lingering trauma that can erode stakeholder trust, damage brand image and increase regulatory scrutiny. Brand managers and consultants are shown in the book how *Corporate Trauma* can severely damage an organization's brand reputation, erode consumer trust, and jeopardize future business ventures and growth.

Cultural Transformation: the shared beliefs, values and behaviors that shape an organization's identity has a profound impact on its performance. *Corporate Trauma* provides a diagnostic framework to better understand chronic corporate underperformance by tracing the problem back to its original cause, that is, the event that triggered the subsequent decline. With this perspective, leadership teams and consultants will be able to examine and respond to the inherited harmful attitudes, behaviors and adaptive cultural routines that contribute to an organization's chronic dysfunctionality.

Strategic Change Management: by recognizing the influence of *Corporate Trauma* on an organization's performance, leadership teams and consultants will be better able to develop more effective strategies for change. Again, by considering the historic nature of a crisis and the often deeply ingrained risk averse cultural norms that have resulted, executives and consultants can take proactive measures to mitigate the effects of inherited trauma and build greater organizational resilience.

Merger & Acquisition Due Diligence: when advising on mergers and acquisitions, consultants thoroughly analyze the target company. This typically includes a financial review (income statements, balance sheets, cash flow) to assess financial health, profitability, and liquidity, ultimately determining fair market value. Beyond financials, the analysis covers tax structure, a legal contract review for liabilities, risks, regulatory compliance, and intellectual property ownership and protection. However, *Corporate Trauma* takes a deep dive into corporate culture, by identifying hidden cultural barriers, such as low employee morale, resistance to change, and issues with productivity and innovation. This framework will help consultants and advisors anticipate integration challenges arising from differing organizational cultures.

Leadership Development Programs: by incorporating the notion of *Corporate Trauma* into leadership development programs, educators can provide students with a more comprehensive understanding of serial corporate turnaround failures and equip them with the tools to develop more effective and sustainable strategies to drive improvements in performance. The case studies in Chapter 5 illustrate how *Corporate Trauma* can manifest in real-world situations. By examining past crises, students can be shown how a stress response to a crisis can trigger leadership changes, cultural shifts and chronic corporate underperformance.

The book is divided into six chapters. **Chapter 1: The Turnaround Playbook Reimagined** argues that a corporate crisis can create a 'hidden trauma' which explains why some firms fail, numerous times, in their attempts to turnaround their fortunes. **Chapter 2: A Brief History of Epigenetics** covers the foundational thinking of Epigenetics and inherited trauma which enables us to evaluate how a corporate crisis can create a trauma that negatively impacts leadership, culture, and performance, thus hindering turnarounds. **Chapter 3: Diagnosing Corporate Trauma** provides a detailed discussion on the methodology and metrics used to identify an inherited trauma in organizations following a corporate crisis. **Chapter 4: Corporate PTSD: When Crises Leave Lasting Scars** takes a deep dive into a number of areas that explains why a corporate crisis can create an adaptive change in culture that triggers a downward spiral in performance and multiple changes in leadership. **Chapter 5: Diagnosing Cases of Corporate Trauma** provides real-world examples of how businesses exposed to a corporate crisis have subsequently produced chronic underperformance. These companies and the crises that they have endured are well known, however, the case studies will offer a new perspective on how these events have created a *Corporate Trauma* that has become embedded in each firm's corporate culture to the detriment of its performance. These case studies offer a valuable 'diagnostic framework' for business leaders, management and consultants to understand the 'root cause' of the trauma and help them identify the underlying reasons for corporate decline. **Chapter 6: The Corporate Trauma Playbook** offers a 'new playbook' that provides a comprehensive guide to manage and, ultimately, overcome the lasting effects and consequences of trauma in an organization. It provides both strategic and tactical solutions to aid recovery and improve corporate performance.

Chapter 2
A Brief History of Epigenetics

Epigenetics is a relatively new field of scientific inquiry which studies how environmental factors can cause genes to switch 'on' or 'off', and importantly how these changes in gene expression are passed down to subsequent generations. The concept of inherited traits has been discussed for centuries with ancient Greek philosophers debating whether or not organisms were fully formed within the egg or developed gradually. In the 18th Century Jean-Baptiste Lamarck, the French naturalist and biologist, attempted to explain how species changed over time through his 'theory of use and disuse'. Published in 1809, Lamarck's book 'Philosophie Zoologique' argued that if an organism repeatedly used a certain feature, that feature became more developed and stronger. Conversely, if a feature was not used, it became weaker and would eventually disappear. For example, he suggested that giraffes developed long necks because they stretched to reach leaves that were in high places on trees, and that this trait was then passed on to their offspring. Whilst his theory was widely accepted for many years, it has since been discredited. In actual fact, modern genetic research has shown that traits are determined primarily by genes, which are passed on from parent to offspring through DNA. While environmental factors can influence gene expression, they cannot directly alter the genes themselves. Despite its flaws, Lamarck's theory helped to lay the groundwork for the modern understanding of how species evolved over time. It also facilitated a shift in the focus from the notion of a 'fixed species' to the idea that species 'changed over time' which paved the way for more accurate theories of evolution, such as Charles Darwin's theory of natural selection which was published in 1859.

It wasn't until the mid-20th century that the term 'epigenetics' was conceived by Conrad H. Waddington, the British biologist, to describe the processes that guided the development of an organism from a single cell. He envisioned an 'epigenetic landscape' where cells could follow different developmental paths based on environmental influences such as diet, stress and exposure to pollutants. This premise has subsequently inspired researchers to undertake studies comparing

https://doi.org/10.1515/9783111571126-002

identical twins, who shared identical DNA, in order to provide evidence for the role of epigenetics in shaping individual differences.[1,2,3]

In biology, an epigenome is a layer of chemical compounds (e.g. methylation and acetylation) that surrounds DNA which can modify the genome without altering the DNA sequence. These compounds are important because they play a key role in determining which genes are active in a particular cell. A common metaphor to describe this epigenetic process is to imagine a piano. The keys represent genes, and the notes they produce represent the traits or characteristics of an organism. The piano itself is the DNA sequence, which remains unchanged. Now, consider the pianist. The pianist's playing style, touch, and interpretation influence the music that is produced. These factors are equivalent to epigenetic modifications. So, in this metaphor, the pianist's playing style (epigenetic modifications) can change the music (traits) produced from the same piano (DNA sequence) and demonstrates how environmental factors can influence gene expression and ultimately shape an organism's characteristics.

9/11's Long Shadow: The Epigenetic Fallout of Disaster

The study of Epigenetics has implications for various fields including medicine, biology, psychology and ecology as it helps explain how the environmental factors experienced by one generation can have long-lasting effects on the health and development of future generations. However, some of these environmental factors (or events) are so traumatic that they can have a profound and enduring effect on an organism, and in the case of the discussion that follows, humans. These effects often extend beyond the immediate aftermath of the event and can manifest in various ways including mental health issues, physical ailments and changes in behavior. Epigenetics provides a potential mechanism for understanding how these enduring effects can occur, and by understanding the molecular mechanisms underlying these effects, researchers have been able to develop more effective interventions to help individuals to improve their health and manage the effects of trauma. For example, the study of epigenetic changes following a traumatic event has helped researchers understand how stress can trigger a cascade of physiological and psychological responses, including the release of stress hormones. An important epigenetic 'marker' is cortisol, a hormone released by the adrenal glands in response to a stressful situation. Cortisol is essential for short-term stress responses as it helps the body prepare for a 'fight-or-flight' reaction by increasing blood sugar, blood pressure and heart rate. However, chronic stress can lead to elevated cortisol levels which can have negative effects on the body, such as, a weakening of the immune system and an increased risk of heart disease and stroke. The relationship between cortisol levels and stress is complex and can vary depending on individual factors. While cortisol levels generally increase in response to stress, they can also be reduced in some individuals with PTSD due to the dysregulation of the hypothalamic-pituitary-adrenal (HPA) axis which controls cortisol production. Exposure to trauma can lead to chronic stress and the functional impairment of the HPA axis which results in either excessive or insufficient cortisol production.

Numerous studies have identified epigenetic alterations in genes associated with individuals who have experienced trauma, and importantly for the study of Corporate Trauma, these epigenetic changes resulted in physical and psychological trauma that had been passed down to several generations of descendants of survivors. This phenomenon is known as an inherited 'transgenerational response'. A transgenerational response to a severe environmental event has been found in numerous studies which indicate that the trauma experienced by one generation can be passed down to subsequent generations through epigenetic mechanisms. For example, a traumatic event experienced by a grandparent could lead to epigenetic modifications that are passed down to their grandchildren which could potentially affect their mental or physical health. A number of research studies have found a transgenerational response to a severe environmental event and include: the inherited effects of maternal malnutrition following exposure to famine which was found to increase the risk of death from cardiovascular disease and diabetes in grandchildren;[4] the off-spring of Australian Vietnam War veterans who suffered from PTSD were found to have a significantly higher risk of developing mental health problems including depression, anxiety and substance abuse, compared to children of non-veterans;[5] the children of survivors of violence and abuse who had an increased risk of mental health problems and substance abuse;[6] and the offspring of World War II holocaust survivors who were found to have an increased susceptibility to stress-related disorders including depression and aggression;[7] and children who had survived a catastrophic earthquake were subsequently found to have brain abnormalities that had been transmitted to their offspring.[8]

September 11th 2001. A date that will resonate with many people as one of the most significant events in recent history following a series of coordinated terrorist attacks that occurred in the United States of America. These attacks had a profound impact on the world at large, leading to significant changes in national security policies and a global 'War on Terror'. This traumatic event also gave rise to a number of illuminating epigenetic studies that identified transgenerational responses in the offspring of survivors. The original premise of these studies reasoned that the potential for a transgenerational response in descendants of people witnessing a catastrophic event that saw two aeroplanes fly into the Twin

Towers of the World Trade Center in New York City, and the subsequent death of nearly 3,000 people, was highly plausible.

One study investigated the relationship between maternal PTSD symptoms and salivary cortisol levels in infants of mothers directly exposed to the devastating effects of the terrorist attack during pregnancy.[9] The study used a combination of biological and psychological measures to investigate the transgenerational effects of PTSD. It involved thirty-eight women who were pregnant and present at, or near, the World Trade Center during the attacks. A longitudinal study of mothers involved completing the Beck Depression Inventory, a 21 question self-report questionnaire that measured the severity of depression; and salivary cortisol samples from each mother and their 1-year old babies upon awakening and at bedtime. The findings were startling and indicated that mothers who developed PTSD exhibited lower cortisol levels compared to similarly exposed mothers who did not develop PTSD. Remarkably, infants of mothers with PTSD also displayed lower salivary cortisol levels during their first year of life. This effect was most pronounced in babies born to mothers who experienced the terrorist attack in their third trimester, but, not in infants born to mothers in the first or second trimesters. This was attributed to stress induced increases in glucocorticoids whose impact is dependent on the gestational age of the foetus. The findings suggest that the effects of maternal PTSD on cortisol can be observed early in the life of offspring and emphasize the significance of 'in-utero' factors as potential biological risk factors for PTSD. Essentially, this study provided a clear example of an inherited transgenerational response and evidence that maternal PTSD can have a significant impact on the health and development of babies, even before birth.

Another study investigated the association between the stress exposure to the World Trade Center attack and air pollution from the dust and gases emitted during the event.[10] The study focused on the birth outcomes of 187 non-smoking women who were pregnant at the time of the event and lived or worked within a 2 mile radius of ground zero. The results of the study, were again, remarkable as they indicated a negative in-utero impact on the health of pregnant women and their foetuses'. Indeed, infants born to women exposed to the attacks during pregnancy were nearly twice as likely to experience in-utero growth restriction, as demonstrated by a significantly lower birth weight (−149g) and birth length (−0.82 cm) compared to infants of unexposed women who were living outside of the Lower Manhattan area. The implications of babies with a lower birth weight have been found to be associated with a range of potential health challenges, both immediate and long-term. In the short term, these infants are more susceptible to complications such as an increased vulnerability to infections, respiratory distress, difficulty maintaining body temperature, and infant mortality. These issues can lead to extended hospital stays and intensive care. Beyond the neonatal period, low birth weight can have lasting consequences in terms of babies experiencing slower growth and development, both physically and cognitively. In the longer term, these children will have an increased risk of chronic health conditions later in life, including heart disease, stroke, diabetes, respiratory problems, and have a permanent vulnerability to depression and stress related illnesses.

The attacks on the World Trade Center on September 11th 2001 continue to provide a fertile ground for epigenetics researchers. Indeed, a recent study examined the physical and mental health of rescue, recovery and clean-up workers who had developed PTSD.[11] The studies discussed above offer a glimpse into the notion of transgenerational response and indicate that the traumatic experiences of ancestors can be passed down to subsequent generations in the form of physical and mental health disorders.

Genes and Generations: The Trauma Connection

As mentioned earlier, the study of epigenetics and inherited trauma is a relatively new field of inquiry, as such, most of the studies to date have focused on parental trauma effects on second generation off-spring. However, there are numerous examples in psychology and sociology literature of historical trauma producing lasting effects on families and communities over many generations. The trauma of slavery, including physical and psychological abuse, has had a profound impact on African American communities for centuries; whilst war, conflict and colonialism produced catastrophic levels of violence, displacement, and cultural oppression which has left a legacy of trauma for generations of survivors. Equally, natural disasters such as hurricanes, earthquakes and tsunamis have had devastating effects on communities, leading to a trauma that has been passed down through multiple generations.

Two key questions emerge from the studies of the exposure to environmental events and their inherited effects. Firstly, how many generations are likely to be affected by the initial traumatic event, and secondly, have these events resulted in inherited changes that have left an 'epigenetic marker' in one generation which has influenced the gene expression in the next generation?

In answer to the first question, scientific studies on rats have become popular because epigenetic changes and inherited trauma can be readily identified due to their relatively short lifespan, ease of breeding, and their genetic similarities to humans. A number of studies have provided valuable insights into how environmental factors such as exposure to parental stress, diet, toxins and drug addiction have resulted in multi-generational changes in physiology and behavior with clear markers relating to altered stress responses.[12,13] Furthermore, compelling evidence for the existence of transgenerational responses to environmental factors in humans was also highlighted in a study that focused on the impact of poor food supply, owing to the failures of crops, on a sample of the population from Överkalix, Sweden, born between 1890 and 1920.[4] Detailed historical records, including parish registers and census data were used to identify and gather information on 271 original participant ancestors and 1,626 participants from second and third generations. The study found that the nutritional status of a grandfather, before puberty, had a significant impact on the health and disease susceptibility, and subsequent lifespan of his grandson. More specifically, the longevity of the grandson was reduced due to 'overeating' which resulted in cardiovascular disease, diabetes and a reduced lifespan. The results of this study provided clear evidence of the link between a traumatic event, that resulted in inherited changes, that left clear 'epigenetic markers' in subsequent generations. As such, the findings supported the hypothesis that a male-line transgenerational response exists in humans, where epigenetic changes were captured in 'nutritionally related information' in subsequent generations of offspring.

Another study of psychosocial stress during pregnancy analyzed the DNA profiles of 121 children linked to grandmaternal exposure to domestic violence. The findings indicated that epigenetic changes in genes had transmitted stress effects to subsequent generations of grandchildren.[14] Whilst not specifically related to epigenetics, the long-term mental health responses to trauma on descendants has also been identified in a number of psychological studies. For example, researchers have not only found anxiety, depression and PTSD in Holocaust survivors, but in both the second (children of survivors) and third (grandchildren of survivors) generations.[15,16] Additionally, research into Joseph Stalin's orchestrated mass starvation of millions of Soviet Ukrainians in the 1930s revealed transgenerational responses on three generations of families who exhibited anxiety, shame, food hoarding, overeating, authoritarian parenting styles and low levels of community trust and cohesiveness.[17]

In summary, the study of Epigenetics is considered to be one of the most important and cutting-edge areas of scientific inquiry as it argues that genes retain historical information which can be passed down through multiple generations. Basically, the assumption is that genes carry the memory of past experiences.[18] The growth in the study of Epigenetics, and in particular research into the transgenerational responses to traumatic events, continues to fascinate researchers from various fields of study that include medicine, biology, psychology and ecology. Indeed, the COVID-19 global pandemic has supercharged the field and we will no doubt see many more studies on inherited trauma in the form of: psychological symptoms (e.g. PTSD, depression, anxiety); biological changes in gene expression; and behavioral patterns in terms of adaptive coping mechanisms that could be passed down to subsequent generations of survivors of the pandemic. Furthermore, the field of epigenetics is undergoing a revolution thanks to rapid progress in sequencing technology, computational biology, and single-cell analysis. These advancements are providing nuanced explanations of complex biological processes and uncovering the intricate mechanisms that 'trigger' epigenetic changes. As these technologies advance, we can anticipate a more comprehensive understanding of epigenetics role in human health, disease, and development. As such, it is plausible to assume that epigenetic research will be extended to 4th and 5th generation (and more) studies into how the negative effects of traumatic events experienced by one generation can create an inherited transgenerational response which is passed down to multiple future generations.

Chapter 3
Diagnosing Corporate Trauma

The idea of Corporate Trauma builds an 'intellectual bridge' and transfer of knowledge between the previously discrete fields of Epigenetics and Business. This bridging process developed a new conceptual framework and methodology that has been underpinned by Epigenetics literature, and in particular, the transgenerational responses to traumatic events. This knowledge has been re-interpreted in the context of business and management literature to explain how a corporate crisis can create a Corporate Trauma that negatively affects organizational leadership, culture and corporate performance in a way that subsequently hinders attempts to successfully turnaround a struggling firm.

In essence, Corporate Trauma uses a diagnostic approach that will enable business leaders and consultants to gain a deeper understanding of the factors contributing to persistent corporate failure and a path out of the maze of uncertainty. This method highlights the importance of considering both internal and external factors when analyzing chronic corporate underperformance and why some firms seem unable to turnaround their fortunes. While traditional approaches to remedy enduring corporate underachievement often focus on external factors such as market conditions or technological advancements, an understanding of Corporate Trauma emphasizes the role of internal factors, such as, corporate culture and leadership in shaping organizational outcomes. As a result, this holistic perspective will allow business leaders and consultants to develop more comprehensive strategies for improving performance, and in particular, for those organizations who struggle with a hidden trauma that has gone unrecognized or unaddressed by a succession of executive leaders. It will enable them to identify and examine any significant crises or setbacks that may have occurred in an organization's history, and to determine if there have been any resulting and dysfunctional cultural adaptations that are not only hindering performance, but importantly, are inherited by successive CEOs. Based on the findings of this diagnostic assessment, executive leaders and consultants will be better able to develop a strategic plan to address any underlying issues and improve performance.

https://doi.org/10.1515/9783111571126-003

We know from the previous discussion on Epigenetics that modifications to gene expression can be passed down from cell to cell and from generation to generation. Researchers have been able to identify these changes by identifying a number of 'epigenetic markers' that help to understand a variety of inherited negative physiological and psychological changes that contribute to ill health, a predisposition to disease, and the subsequent poorer development of generations of an organism. In the development of metrics to diagnose Corporate Trauma, the studies relating to the World Trade Center attacks were, in particular, important since the results concluded that the enduring effects on participants manifested in the form of physiological changes (mothers and babies with lower cortisol levels; and babies with significantly lower average birth weight and size) and psychological changes (mothers with PTSD and depression, and children with a permanent vulnerability to stress related illnesses).

An organization under stress often displays a range of signs, each a symptom of deeper underlying issues. These indicators include a decline in employee morale, increased absenteeism, decreased productivity, and a general sense of apathy leading to high staff turnover rates. Furthermore, an organization under stress may experience a decline in innovation and creativity with employees feeling overwhelmed and anxious to the point where they struggle to think outside the box and come up with new ideas. This can stifle growth and hinder the organization's ability to adapt to changing circumstances, which in turn, leads to decreased revenue, increased costs, and difficulty meeting financial obligations. This deterioration and downward spiral in the health and financial performance of an organization often results in cost-cutting, layoffs, reduced benefits, and a general sense of insecurity among employees.

The 'Markers' of Corporate Trauma

In diagnosing Corporate Trauma in organizations, a number of physiological markers (Market Capitalization, Revenue, Operating Income, R&D Expenditure, R&D Intensity, and CEO turnover) and a single psychological marker (corporate attitudes to innovation and risk) have been used to identify and quantify how an environmental factor (corporate crisis) can create an adverse modification in an organization (corporate culture) that affects its health and development (corporate financial performance) which is then passed on to multiple generations (CEO leadership) and hinders attempts to successfully turnaround a firm.

The analysis of the markers of Corporate Trauma was undertaken by comparing the data from *'before and after a corporate crisis'* to understand the short-term effects and longer-term consequences of such events. The average % increase or decrease in each physiological marker in the years before and after the crisis has been used to illustrate the resulting change or adaptation in an organization. Comparing the 'average' percentage change in the key markers enables us to identify trends and patterns that might not be apparent in a simple year-by-year comparison. This approach is particularly useful in mitigating the impact of short-term volatility, which can often obscure underlying trends. By way of illustration, if a corporate crisis occurred in 2006, the Market Capitalisation of the firm in that year was compared with the 'average' Market Capitalisation figure in the years prior to and following the crisis event. By implication, a comparison of Market Capitalization before and after a crisis will pinpoint the extent to which the event has affected investor confidence. A significant decline in Market Capitalization following a crisis may indicate that investors perceive the company to be at increased risk, leading to a loss of firm value. Conversely, a recovery in Market Capitalization may signal that the company has successfully weathered the storm and regained investor trust. Similarly, by examining changes in other financial markers such as Revenue and Operating Income, we can gain an insight into the broader impact of a crisis on a company's financial health and development. An increase in these metrics may indicate that the crisis hasn't disrupted the company's operations, whilst a decrease may suggest that the company is yet to recover fully. However, it is important to note that the impact of a crisis can vary significantly from company to company and factors such as the severity of the crisis, the company's financial strength, and its ability to respond effectively to the event can all influence the outcome.

The following discussion provides a detailed explanation of the key markers, metrics and methodological approach that have been used to identify Corporate Trauma in the illustrative case studies provided in Chapter 5: Diagnosing Cases of Corporate Trauma.

1. A Corporate Crisis (environmental factor):
A corporate crisis can arise from a variety of sources including natural disasters, technological failures, public health emergencies, financial scandals, supply chain disruptions, faulty products and their subsequent recall. In fact, the list is almost endless. The idea of Corporate Trauma argues that a crisis event acts as a 'trigger' causing a downward spiral in the performance of an organization. Crucially, the crisis event can be distinctly identified as happening on a specific date, like the World Trade Centre attacks on September 11th 2001, or over an epoch defining period such as The Holocaust of World War II which occurred between 1933 and

1945. As such, a corporate crisis should be referred to as a 'Critical Corporate Incident (CCI)' as all crisis events have the potential to create a profound impact on an organization. These events are 'critical' if they are clearly identifiable and result in subsequent corporate 'effects' and 'consequences' which influence the health and development of an organization. Whilst the terms 'effects' and 'consequences' are often used interchangeably, there is a subtle difference between them, in so far as, an effect focuses on the direct and immediate result of a corporate crisis, whilst the consequence of this event emphasizes the long-term implications of the crisis.

The notion of a CCI draws on Critical Incident Theory, a powerful research methodology that has been used extensively in business and management research to identify a significant event that subsequently influences organizational behavior, employee experiences and leadership behavior.[1,2] By focusing on significant events we are better able to uncover important patterns and themes in organizational dynamics that may not be apparent through other research methods. This line of reasoning aligns with epigenetics research which argues that a severe environmental event can result in detrimental effects and consequences on the development and health of future generations. Whilst the critical incident method is a valuable tool that can reveal adaptive changes in organizational attitudes and behaviours, it should be acknowledged that the selection of companies in the illustrative case studies that follow in Chapter 5 is subjective. However, they do provide a strong argument for an inherited stress reaction and a transgenerational response in the form of Corporate Trauma effects and consequences.

2. Corporate Culture (an adverse modification in an organization)

With many consultants and researchers referring to corporate culture in terms of 'Corporate DNA'[3,4,5] it's not that farfetched to believe in the notion of a transgenerational response in relation to a corporate crisis. Corporate culture is widely regarded as the collective cognition of implied assumptions and shared beliefs that differentiate one organization from another. It also creates a tacit social order that shapes and regulates attitudes, behaviors and social norms toward a shared organizational goal that aims to enhance performance through the aspirational commitment of employees. However, many consultants and researchers have noted that organizations can be held captive by their culture as its values and beliefs act as an invisible barrier against change and hinders efforts to promote adaptation and transformation.

The dominant view in business and management literature is that corporate culture is difficult to measure due to the often hidden, unconscious and subjective ways of working within an organization. Traditional approaches to measuring corporate culture have combined quantitative (e.g. employee satisfaction and engagement surveys) and qualitative methods (e.g. observing employee interactions, focus groups) to gain an understanding of culture and how to improve it. Measuring the full extent of corporate culture is a complex and nuanced process and the approach used to identify Corporate Trauma focuses on two aspects of culture that play a fundamental role in influencing corporate performance, that is, organizational attitudes and behaviours relating to 'innovation' and 'risk'. Some firms are known to be more 'culturally orientated' toward innovation and embed it into the DNA of their business through consistent investments in R&D, that in the long run, delivers new products and services and improved market performance. Indeed, an organization's R&D-led innovation growth strategy is largely based on an assessment of 'risk' with CEOs and their executive leadership team often evaluating risk alternatives that range from having a 'certain outcome' to 'taking a gamble'. However, a corporate crisis can severely curtail a firm's investment in innovation as the immediate focus shifts towards damage control and restoring its reputation. In the short-term, the focus on crisis management can lead to an emphasis on immediate survival rather than future growth. This can stifle creativity and discourage risk-taking, both of which are essential for fostering innovation. In addition, funds that were previously earmarked for R&D are diverted to address the pressing needs of the crisis with significant resources re-allocated to crisis management teams, legal counsel, and public relations efforts. In the longer-term, a crisis can erode investor confidence, leading to a decline in market capitalization and a decrease in available capital which makes it more challenging for companies to secure funding for innovative projects. In essence, a crisis event can act as a 'trigger' that creates dysfunctional adaptive changes in attitudes and behaviors that subsequently become embedded in the culture of an organization to the detriment of its long-term viability and performance. For this reason, corporate attitudes to innovation and risk are considered to be a key psychological 'marker' of Corporate Trauma, and as such, these adaptive changes in culture need to be tracked over time in order to clearly identify how an organization's culture has evolved in response to a crisis.

The premise and evidence presented in this book argues that the Corporate Trauma and adverse cultural adaptations resulting from a crisis can be measured by using the following metrics. Firstly, a quantitative and longitudinal *Content Analysis* of the 'word frequencies' contained in corporate annual reports can identify any cultural adaptation in terms of an organization's attitudes to innovation and risk. The premier software package NVivo was used to identify meaningful data from the text rich annual reports in order to recognise patterns in a range of words associated with the terms 'innovation' and 'risk' (see Appendix 1 for a detailed list). Descriptive statistics were then used to calculate the frequency of each word, in relation to the total number of words in each report, to produce a trend over the period 2000 to 2024. Whilst the use of corporate annual reports is often criticized for their inherent bias, often associated with CEO narcissism, the embedded cultural traits contained in annual reports are a rich source of data that meets the legal demands of investors, stakeholders and regulatory bodies. As such, they are a consistent and reliable source of data on an organization's direction, performance and compliance. Secondly, *R&D Expenditure* is an investment in future innovation. This metric can provide valuable insights into a firm's performance with high spending demonstrating a commitment to innovation and developing new products and services and improved operational efficiency that contributes to overall financial performance. This metric also signals a focus on long-term success, rather than just short-term profits and indicates a firm's intention to remain relevant and adapt to future market changes. Thirdly, *R&D Intensity* is a direct measure of a firm's enthusiasm for innovation and is a forward-looking metric that reflects a commitment to future growth. By investing in R&D, organizations can improve processes and efficiency, and build a sustainable pipeline of patents and innovative products and services to generate higher levels of growth. Consequently, by quantifying the proportion of resources allocated to R&D activities we can gain a clear indication of a firm's innovation-led growth strategies and benchmark this against the innovation levels of different firms and industries. R&D Intensity is calculated by dividing a firm's Sales Revenue by its R&D Expenditure to derive a percentage figure and is a metric that has been found to indicate that higher levels of R&D activity in relation to sales revenue is a good measure of long-term corporate performance.[6,7] Unfortunately, R&D Expenditure has not been identified in the financial returns of AIG, Barclays and Wells Fargo & Company and so a calculation of R&D Intensity is not possible. According to the International Financial Reporting Standards accounting rules, the level of R&D activity is reported as 'inactive' because these financial firms believe the expenditure is so 'immaterial' that it is combined with other intangible assets in financial reporting. AIG, Barclays and Wells Fargo & Company are not exceptional cases, since certain industries have different norms and practices regarding R&D disclosure. For example, industries that rely heavily on innovation, such as technology or pharmaceuticals, tend to be more transparent about their R&D spending, whereas companies operating in financial services tend to allocate a small portion of their overall expenses to R&D, therefore, making these costs negligeable for reporting purposes.

3. Corporate Financial Performance (the health and development of an organization)

Corporate culture drives long-term performance, with firms being either open, or resistant, to the idea of innovation. Developing a strategic outlook, investments, systems, people and processes that deliver innovative new products and services valued by customers is essentially a choice. The corporate performance of firms exposed to a crisis has focused on how an organization is currently performing when compared with its past achievements. Once again, the data was analysed in terms of what happened *before and after the corporate crisis?* As with the babies born to mothers who were exposed to the 9/11 terrorist attacks, the corporate financial performance of firms experiencing a crisis would equally be traumatic. The historic financial data used in the illustrative case studies that follow was obtained from S&P Capital IQ. This database provides comprehensive and robust financial analysis and is widely used by a range of investment, corporate finance and consulting professionals to analyze market trends, conduct industry analysis and benchmark corporate financial performance.

The following metrics have been used to analyze corporate financial performance:

Market Capitalization is a collective measure of the market sentiment of investors on a firm's current and future potential in terms of strategy, growth, investment goals and profitability. An increasing figure suggests that investors believe the company has strong growth potential, while a decreasing one indicates less optimism about its future. Whilst this metric is not a perfect measure of corporate performance, previous studies have shown a correlation between a high market capitalization and corporate performance.[8,9] Furthermore, companies with higher market capitalizations are often perceived as more innovative and likely to generate future growth due to their greater financial stability and access to capital. Whilst many evaluations of corporate performance compares current with past achievements, this internal view needs to be considered in the context of measuring 'comparative' firm performance against industry leaders, specific competitors, and best practice firms in other sectors. This external approach to corporate benchmarking aims to understand a firm's performance against 'best-in-class' organizations to identify gaps, strengths and weaknesses in the company's performance in order to identify areas for improvement and gain a competitive edge. As such, an analysis of market capitalization allows for an easy comparison of companies within the same industry or across different sectors which enables investors to identify relative performance and assess whether a company is outperforming or underperforming its peers. Consequently, the S&P Global 1200 Index has been used to benchmark the corporate performance of all companies presented in the case studies in Chapter 5. This index tracks the performance of the world's leading publicly traded companies in 31 countries and accounts for around 70% of the entire global stock market capitalization. It is made up of 7 regional indices: S&P 500 (US), S&P Europe 350, S&P TOPIX 150 (Japan), S&P/TSX 60 (Canada), S&P/ASX All Australian 50, S&P Asia 50 and S&P

Latin America 40. Essentially, the S&P Global 1200 is the 'go to' index for organizations seeking to achieve continuous improvement in corporate performance and benchmark this against world-class performers.

Revenue from sales is a key metric for measuring corporate performance, offering valuable insights into an organization's ability to generate income from its core operations and attract customers. Higher revenue translates into greater financial resources for the company, particularly in terms of the opportunity to invest in R&D initiatives. Furthermore, the assessment of revenue data can be used to identify market growth opportunities and inform strategic decisions relating to new product launches and marketing campaigns which tends to boost investor confidence, leading to increased stock prices and easier access to capital. Furthermore, revenue is a key metric that is used to evaluate the performance of executives, managers, and employees and can be used to set performance targets and incentivize desired organizational attitudes and behaviors.

Operating Income offers a compelling measure of a company's financial performance due to its ability to understand how core business operations generate profits. This is particularly valuable when comparing companies with different capital structures or tax jurisdictions, as it removes these external factors. Moreover, operating income is a useful tool for assessing a company's operational efficiency and the robustness of its business model, with consistent increases in this metric indicating that an organization is effectively executing its business strategy and is well-positioned for future success.

4. CEO Leadership (A Transgenerational Response)

A 'corporate generation' is an idea that has not been fully established in business and management literature. Whilst some studies have focussed on the 'evolution of corporate codes of ethics'[10] and how a 'customised management strategy' is essential for motivating diverse employees across multiple age generations[11], the idea that it is the 'tenure' of a CEO that determines a corporate generation is a new concept. However, there is a strong argument to say that a corporate generation starts with the appointment of a new CEO and ends when that executive is replaced. The appointment of a new CEO can have significant implications for the organization, its employees, and its stakeholders since a new CEO often brings a fresh perspective and a new strategic vision. This can lead to significant changes in the company's strategic direction, goals and priorities, which in turn, is likely to result in changes to organizational structure, the reallocation of resources and streamlining processes. Furthermore, a new CEO can have a profound impact on an organization's cultural DNA by introducing new values, behaviors and expectations which can lead to significant changes in the workplace.

Several longitudinal studies by The Harvard Law School Forum on Corporate Governance have examined the 'CEO Succession Practices' amongst U.S. public companies from 2000 to 2020. These studies analyzed factors such as the correlation between CEO succession and company performance, the age, tenure and qualifications of incoming and departing CEOs. The most recent study reported that the average CEO tenure in S&P 500 companies during 2020 was 9.3 years, which is a figure that is consistent with comparisons dating back to 2014.[12] So, by implication, a CEO's tenure that is less than this 'average figure' could be indicative of an underperforming leader and their ability to improve the performance of the firm. The calculation of CEO tenure involves dividing the number of full financial years of service for each CEO by the aggregate number of CEOs who assumed the role subsequent to the crisis year. As such, the examination of transgenerational responses over multiple corporate generations is identified by the key marker of CEO turnover and is supported with thematic analysis of CEO letters to shareholders as they offer a unique perspective into a company's strategic direction, financial performance, and overall health. These letters also tend to highlight a company's strengths and weaknesses relative to its rivals and insights into potential threats, risks and opportunities so that investors can assess the company's resilience and future prospects. Furthermore, the tone and content of these letters can also offer a glimpse into a new CEO's leadership philosophy and management style and provide an insight into organizational culture.

The discussion that follows in Chapter 4: Corporate PTSD: When Crises Leave Lasting Scars takes a deep dive into the 'key markers' of Corporate Trauma. As such, a thorough and in-depth examination of widely cited studies in business and management literature will provide a comprehensive understanding into how chronic corporate underperformance can result from a crisis event that has subsequently had a profound and transgenerational impact on an organization's culture, financial performance and CEO tenure.

Chapter 4
Corporate PTSD: When Crises Leave Lasting Scars

Historically, corporate turnaround strategies have primarily focused on short-term financial activities, such as, cost-cutting and restructuring the configuration and operations of an underperforming organization. However, the following narrative suggests a more nuanced perspective that challenges the prevailing assumption that organizations can easily overcome adversity and improve performance. It proposes that chronic corporate underperformance could be a symptom of a historic organizational trauma. A significant crisis event can leave lasting scars on an organization that manifests in a persistent aversion to risk, a reluctance to embrace innovation, and a general inability to adapt to changing market conditions. In essence, just as individuals can suffer from PTSD, organizations too may experience a similar condition.

Corporate crises can have far-reaching consequences, extending beyond immediate financial losses and reputational damage. These events can 'trigger' a downward spiral, leading to a long-term decline in the health, development and performance of an organization. The impact of a crisis is not solely determined by the severity of the event itself, but also by how it is perceived and managed. A key factor influencing the long-term consequences of a crisis is the perception of 'intentionality'. Intentional wrongdoing, such as fraud or deception, can erode trust and damage a company's reputation irreparably. Conversely, unintentional crises, such as product recalls or natural disasters, may be more easily forgiven if handled appropriately. The role of leadership in navigating crises is paramount, with CEOs in particular, playing a crucial role in shaping an organization's response and guiding it through the crisis.

The previous discussion in Chapter 3: Diagnosing Corporate Trauma will now be extended to a deep dive into the relevant business and management literature in order to frame the transgenerational effects and consequences of a crisis on an organization. The following discussion will explore the multifaceted impact of a corporate crisis by examining how Corporate Trauma can prompt adaptive changes in an organization's leadership, culture, financial performance which, ultimately, influences its ability to fully recover. Several factors have previously been identified as crucial when addressing the key 'markers' of Corporate Trauma and these will now be discussed in more detail to reveal how a crisis can cause chronic dysfunction in an organization.

https://doi.org/10.1515/9783111571126-004

From Scandal to Stagnation: The Toxic Legacy of Corporate Misdeeds

Chronic corporate underperformance occurs over a sustained period of time as a result of external factors such as economic conditions, regulatory changes, and industry disruptions; and internal factors in the form of the strategic misalignment of market demands with internal capabilities, poor leadership, a resistance to change from employees, and a lack of investment in R&D to drive the development of innovative new products and services. These crisis events can trigger a downward spiral that, if not effectively managed, can lead to long-term decline in the health and development of an organization. For example, crises in the form of defective products in the U.S. automobile industry, and their subsequent recall, were found to produce short-term negative effects on consumer preference which led to an immediate decrease in sales, revenue and an instant fall in a firm's share price. Furthermore, large product recalls can take longer to settle and involve significantly more costs due to potential lawsuits and fines by regulatory bodies. This subsequently sends an adverse signal to investors, who tend to overreact negatively to recall announcements, compounding their pessimism about the brand and the firm's future, leading to a long-term decline in market capitalization.[1] The impact of a corporate crisis on a firm's reputation and value is more nuanced than one might think. How stakeholders initially react to news of a crisis has been found to depend on a number of factors including an acknowledgement of responsibility, perceptions of intentionality, the severity of the crisis, and ability to control and minimize the damage. The intricate relationship between corporate reputation and firm value was examined in a longitudinal study of 126 crises which revealed that high levels of brand equity were found to act as buffer against firm value loss.[2] The study's findings also revealed that while both brand 'familiarity' and 'favorability' contributed to a company's reputation, their effects on firm value during a crisis differed. Notably, a company's familiarity appeared to be a double-edged sword. On one hand, it amplified the negative impact of a crisis, as a well-known company attracts greater media attention and public scrutiny. On the other, familiarity of a brand can also mitigate against the impact of the crisis due to a pre-existing reservoir of goodwill and trust that can help lessen the blow. In contrast, favorability, or the extent to which stakeholders viewed a company positively, emerged as a more consistent and powerful driver of protecting firm value during a crisis. Companies with strong reputations for ethical behavior, social responsibility, and customer satisfaction tended to weather a crisis more effectively. This suggests that investing in building a positive corporate image can yield significant long-term benefits, particularly in times of turmoil.

The perceived 'intentionality' of the cause of a corporate crisis also plays a pivotal role in determining stakeholder responses. Cases of corporate fraud and deception, for example, Enron (2001), WorldCom (2002), Lehman Brothers (2008) and Theranos (2015) were found to be intentional, with the illegal and unethical actions committed by individuals motivated purely by personal and corporate gain. The perception of intentionality in these cases, ultimately, led to heightened negative stakeholder emotions, reduced brand loyalty, diminished purchase intentions and an erosion of trust. Even the most reputable companies will struggle to recover if the cause of the crisis is seen as intentional, and whilst a strong reputation can act as an initial safeguard, it cannot completely shield a company from the consequences of intentional wrongdoing.[3]

The findings of these studies have important implications for the examination of Corporate Trauma, in so far as, corporate crises can have a lasting negative impact on a firm's reputation, even years after the initial event due to the perceived intentional wrongdoing. Whilst the immediate effects of a corporate crisis include reputational damage and a loss of trust among stakeholders, the longer-term consequences often result in decreased sales, increased costs, and potentially expensive legal settlements. Financial losses often follow which can diminish an organization's resources and make it difficult to invest in growth and innovation opportunities. This in turn can make it difficult for an organization to compete effectively in its market, leading to a decline in market share, profitability, and overall performance. The stress and uncertainty caused by the short-term effects and longer-term consequences of a crisis can also lead to a 'cultural erosion' that is exhibited in a decline in employee morale, productivity and an exodus of top talent which further hinders business performance. The overall consequence of a crisis is organizational stagnation, and in such circumstances, corporate turnaround becomes a critical imperative.

From the Brink: The Fight for Corporate Survival

Chronic corporate underperformance is often measured by a number of metrics that demonstrate signs of financial distress, such as declining profitability, negative cash flow and high debt levels. Importantly, these metrics when compared to industry benchmarks and historical firm trends are likely to indicate an organization's poor comparative performance in terms of revenue and market share. A period of three or more consecutive years of poor financial returns is widely considered to be a key 'marker' of chronic corporate underperformance that threatens the survival of a firm.[4,5] Those organizations that appear unable to achieve sustained profitability and reverse the decline in performance are considered as a potential turnaround case.

The classic turnaround playbook typically involves two phases. Phase 1 will see the appointment of new leadership, often with a mandate to revitalize a failing business by managing costs, restructuring the organization, maximizing cash flow and debt restructuring to restore profitability. As such, reducing the size of the workforce, and curtailing R&D and marketing expenditure helps to stabilize the distressed firm's finances. Phase 2 usually involves developing a broad vision for growth and setting a new strategic direction that aims to generate employee and stakeholder enthusiasm.

However, a corporate turnaround is not merely a financial exercise. It requires a comprehensive approach that addresses both operational and cultural issues. A successful turnaround involves not only stabilizing the company's finances but also revitalizing its workforce and fostering a culture of innovation and adaptability. Newly appointed CEOs also need to win the hearts and minds of employees and other stakeholders. Resistance to change is a common obstacle, and new leadership must effectively engage and communicate a new vision for the future and change organizational culture to foster a more positive, productive, and innovative environment. Another critical aspect of corporate turnaround is strategic repositioning. In some cases, the company may need to diversify into new markets to address changing consumer preferences or industry trends. This requires careful planning and execution to ensure that any new ventures align with the company's core competencies and strategic objectives. Time constraints are also a significant challenge in corporate turnaround. The need to act quickly to prevent further deterioration of the company's financial situation can put pressure on management to make rapid decisions, which may increase the risk of strategic and operational mistakes.

A corporate turnaround is a period of significant strategic change that is initiated in response to a sustained decline in business performance. This change is a complex and challenging undertaking even for the most experienced senior executives and management consultants as it can involve a variety of actions, such as restructuring the company's operations, divesting non-core assets, or acquiring new businesses. As such, a successful turnaround requires a combination of strong leadership, effective strategies, and a commitment to a change process over several years.

The Roots of Chronic Corporate Underperformance

By understanding the characteristics of turnaround firms, the role of leadership, and the challenges and success factors involved, organizations can increase their chances of successfully navigating difficult times and achieving long-term sustainability. However, finding a way out of the maze of Corporate Trauma is often a complex interplay of factors, making it challenging to pinpoint a singular cause. One of the primary challenges in recognizing the causes of corporate decline lies in the inherent biases and blind spots that can afflict organizations. Overconfidence in past successes can lead to complacency and a reluctance to adapt to changing market conditions. Similarly, a focus on short-term gains may neglect long-term investments in R&D, innovation, and talent development. Additionally, organizational cultures that prioritize conformity over dissent may stifle creativity and critical thinking, hindering the ability to identify and address emerging threats. Ultimately, recognizing the *'root cause'* of chronic underperformance can be challenging because it is largely hidden from view.

The idea of Corporate Trauma argues that the fundamental reason for an organization's chronic underperformance could well be a historic crisis event that has had long-term consequences for a firm which have extended far beyond the initial public relations, financial and operational challenges. Identifying the root cause of an organization's decline is crucial for effective problem-solving; treating the symptoms of a problem, without addressing the root cause, is like putting a band-aid on a bullet wound. It might temporarily alleviate the pain, but it won't solve the underlying issue.

When a Corporate Crisis creates a 'Hidden' Trauma

The traditional approach to corporate crisis management focuses on short-term measures to address the immediate effects of the crisis. The prevailing view of managing corporate crisis situations is that an effective resolution is often achieved by adopting a systematic approach which aims to anticipate, prevent, and mitigate the negative impact of unexpected events that threaten an organization's reputation, financial stability, and operations.[6,7,8] As such, a well-structured crisis management plan is essential as it outlines the roles and responsibilities of key personnel, establishes communication protocols, and provides a framework for adaptive decision-making during times of turbulence. One of the most critical aspects of crisis management is risk assessment. By identifying potential threats and evaluating their likelihood and impact, organizations can prioritize their preparedness efforts and allocate resources accordingly. Risk assessments consider a wide range of factors, including natural disasters, cybersecurity threats, supply chain disruptions, and reputational damage. Once potential risks have been identified, organizations can develop strategies to mitigate their impact. This may involve implementing preventative measures, such as investing in appropriate insurance cover, conducting regular training, and maintaining contingency plans. When a crisis occurs, it is essential to respond quickly and decisively in order to preserve the trust of a range of stakeholders that include customers, investors, and the public. In addition, it is also important to maintain open and honest communication with employees by providing timely information and support to help alleviate anxiety and maintain morale.

CEO Leadership: The key to Navigating Corporate Crises

Given that older CEOs have been found to be less cognitively nimble than their younger counterparts, another important question presents itself in terms of their ability to manage a severe corporate crisis and potentially the lasting negative trauma effects on an organization. A corporate crisis can be a devastating event for a company, potentially leading to significant financial losses, reputational damage, and even legal consequences. In such chaotic times, the CEO's role becomes both paramount and multi-faceted. They are the face of the company, responsible for guiding the organization through the crisis and restoring public trust. When a crisis strikes, the CEO must quickly assess the situation, implement a comprehensive response plan, and communicate effectively with all stakeholders to mitigate panic, maintain morale, and prevent the situation from escalating. Furthermore, the CEO's public image is inextricably linked to the company's reputation, and during a crisis, it is essential for them to be transparent, empathetic, and accountable. By taking ownership of the situation and addressing concerns head-on, the CEO can help to rebuild trust and prevent further damage. Once the immediate crisis has been addressed, they must focus on long-term recovery, building resilience and implementing new policies and procedures to prevent similar crises from happening in the future.

Past Crises, Future Performance: Understanding the Corporate Trauma Effect

Crisis management is not just about responding to emergencies; it is also about learning from past experiences and improving future preparedness. After a crisis, organizations will conduct a thorough review to identify lessons learned and make necessary adjustments to their crisis management plans. This ongoing process of evaluation and improvement is essential for building resilience and ensuring that the organization is well-prepared to face future challenges.

This approach to corporate crisis management is valid and has been tested in the heat of battle during many crises over many decades. However, it is a short-term view and one that ignores the potential for a crisis to create long-term and 'hidden' consequences for firms that hinder their ability to fully recover. In the same way that epigenetics researchers have found that severe environmental events can create negative transgenerational responses in the health and development of an organism, the experience of a corporate crisis can lead to organizational stress and anxiety that creates a long-term Corporate Trauma in the form of deep-rooted cultural and psychological effects that can have an impact on employees at all levels of an organization. This trauma can include feelings of shock, disbelief, and fear. Over time, these unresolved emotional reactions can manifest as a 'collective trauma' within the organization which is often overlooked or minimized in a crisis management response. This hidden trauma can manifest in various ways, such as decreased employee morale, reduced productivity, increased absenteeism, and difficulty making decisions. It can also lead to a breakdown in trust between employees and management, hindering collaboration and communication. Furthermore, the trauma can create an adaptive and negative change in organizational culture that is characterized by fear, blame, and avoidance. Ultimately, the trauma can have long-lasting negative consequences for the company's health, development and performance which can leave it vulnerable to future shocks and setbacks.

The idea of Corporate Trauma argues that by recognizing the hidden trauma that can result from a corporate crisis, organizations can mitigate its negative effects and consequences and create a more resilient and healthy work environment by implementing organizational changes to address the root causes of the trauma. The first step is to acknowledge the existence of dysfunctional adaptive responses, inherited attitudes and behaviors that have become embedded in the corporate culture to the detriment of the long-term viability and performance of the firm. For example, a firm that has been exposed to a traumatic event would likely be more risk averse, and so evidence of this would be found in documents relating to organizational policies, strategies, processes and procedures; and indicated by reductions in R&D spending or wholesale workforce cuts.[9]

The Cultural Scars of Crisis: When Trauma Shapes Organizational DNA

The literature on corporate culture reveals a diverse subject field with many definitions and numerous theoretical frameworks that seek to explain the phenomenon. The foundational thinking on corporate culture emerged in the 1950s with research into the cultural aspects of 'conflict on organizational unity' and how a cross-cultural context influenced 'the patterns of organizational behavior' required to achieve organizational adaptation.[10,11] Whilst the literature of the 1970s coalesced around the term 'Corporate Culture' it wasn't until the 1980s that the topic received serious attention and a remarkable growth in the number of studies that continued to evolve by examining a diverse range of topics. These include highly cited work on culture as a pattern of shared assumptions that operate unconsciously within an organization, and specifically: the role of people in creating organizational climate and culture;[12] the role of leadership in developing organizational culture;[13] and how leaders play a crucial role in shaping and maintaining corporate culture in high-performing organizations.[14]

Corporate culture is often described as the 'personality' of a company. It is a complex tapestry of shared beliefs, values, attitudes, and behaviors that define how an organization operates. It's the invisible force that shapes everything from employee morale and productivity, to customer satisfaction and overall business performance. At its core, an organization's culture creates a shared sense of purpose and belonging that fosters a climate where employees feel valued, motivated, and empowered to contribute their best. An important aspect of an organization's culture is a shared commitment to the fundamental values that guide it's behavior. These values are often communicated to all employees and reinforced through policies, practices and rewards. A strong culture can help to attract and retain top talent, improve employee engagement, and enhance creativity and innovation. Conversely, a negative or toxic culture can lead to high staff turnover, low employee morale and decreased productivity.

This traditional view of reducing corporate culture to a set of shared values or beliefs is widely accepted, however, a closer examination of culture reveals a more complex phenomenon, shaped by a myriad of factors including history, leadership, structure, and an organization's competitive environment. A more nuanced view of culture differentiates between ideology and culture and suggests that ideology is the official, often idealized version of a company's values and beliefs, whilst culture emphasizes the role of rituals and symbols in shaping employee attitudes and behaviors. Rituals, such as company meetings or award ceremonies, reinforce shared values and norms. Symbols, such as logos or uniforms, represent the organization's identity and can have a powerful impact on employee morale and commitment.[15] This emphasis on the interplay between ideology, rituals, symbols, and leadership provides a rich and subtle understanding of how culture shapes organizational behavior and performance.

One of the biggest challenges for an organization is maintaining a positive culture in the face of change, or indeed, a crisis. As the competitive environment becomes increasingly dynamic and uncertain, companies must be able to adapt and evolve, which can be a difficult process when employees are resistant to change. While culture can enhance performance through employee commitment, it can also become a barrier to change particularly when ingrained values and beliefs hinder adaptation. The key question that Corporate Trauma addresses is to understand whether or not a past corporate crisis has led to a hidden and dysfunctional cultural adaptation where negative attitudes and behaviors have subsequently become entrenched in the culture of the firm to the detriment of its long-term viability and performance?

Corporate DNA: Culture Drives Performance

An extensive body of business and management literature considers an organization's culture to be the 'DNA of a firm'.[16,17,18,19] In terms of drawing a parallel with an organization's culture, DNA carries the genetic information that allows an organism to function, grow and reproduce. However, there is a tension that exists in our current understanding of how corporate culture changes and evolves. On the one hand, a dominant view in literature suggests that culture is flexible and evolves in response to external and internal change agents. As with an organism's DNA, it is adaptable and subject to change as a result of a mutation caused by exposure to an environmental factor. Conversely, an opposing view argues that organizations can be 'captured' by their culture which makes it difficult to manage and control it's direction and performance. Tom Peters, the renowned management consultant, illustrated this point by arguing that "all the behavior of an enterprise is pretty much direct inheritance of its gene pool".[20] By comparing an organization to a biological organism, his suggestion was that an organization's culture was similar to a genetic code that deeply influenced its behavior and actions. Just as the genetic makeup of an individual determines their physical traits and predispositions, a corporate culture is shaped by its values, beliefs, and overall approach to business. As such, an organization's culture is not something that can be easily changed or manipulated. It is deeply ingrained and often passed down from generation to generation of leadership, management, and employees. This suggests that efforts to transform corporate culture must be strategic and long-term, rather than superficial or short-lived. Furthermore, the gene pool analogy highlights the importance of understanding an organization's history and traditions. These elements, like the genetic makeup of an individual, can provide valuable insights into the organization's current behavior and future potential. By recognizing the cultural underpinnings of an organization, leaders can make more informed decisions and foster a more effective and sustainable business. C-suite executives play a pivotal role in shaping corporate culture by setting a strong example through their own conduct. By exhibiting actions and behaviors that can create a positive and supportive culture, senior executives can foster a climate where employees are highly engaged and deliver on organizational values and objectives.

A significant body of literature also indicates that an existing culture tends to discourage organizational change and encourages perpetuation of the status quo, primarily due to embedded values and beliefs which act as an invisible barrier against change.[21,22,23] As such, organizations develop a dominant logic which creates a tacit social order that favors a consistency in cultural norms and deters change. These views are interesting when considering the impact of a crisis event on an organization's culture and performance. Epigenetics literature argues that severe environmental conditions can result in negative and often chronic changes in physiological and psychological characteristics. So in the face of a corporate crisis, two crucial questions arise. Firstly, does a crisis result in an evolutionary cultural adaptation in the firm, or does it result in a no change scenario because the organization is being held prisoner to a path dependent culture? Secondly, does an evolutionary cultural adaptation in response to a corporate crisis have a lasting impact on an organization's health, development and performance, and in particular, its ability to innovate and adapt to future challenges?

The Role of Culture in Driving Innovation

The intricate relationship between organizational culture, innovation, risk and performance has been a subject of growing interest in the practitioner and academic communities. While research in this area is still relatively nascent, a consensus is emerging that these elements are inextricably linked since an innovative culture has been found to be a good measure of an organization's orientation toward innovation; and its ability to adopt new ideas and processes that often leads to new products and services, and eventually, improved market performance.[24,25]

Understanding this relationship is crucial for organizations seeking to enhance their performance and competitiveness, however, some firms are known to be culturally more open, or resistant, to the idea of innovation and developing (or not) the strategic outlook, policies, investments, systems, people and processes that deliver imaginative new products and services. Indeed, the Boston Consulting Group's survey of the world's 'Most Innovative Companies' in 2023 highlights the importance of an organizational culture that values experimentation and learning, and regards failure as a fundamental step in driving innovation. The findings indicate that the most innovative companies share one thing in common – they have a culture that actively fosters innovation and quickly transforms R&D activity into valuable growth opportunities. The survey also found that innovation had surged to the top of corporate agendas in 2023, with 79% of companies ranking it as a top-three priority (up from 75% in 2022) with leading companies making it the cornerstone of their future growth strategies. Indeed, "innovation ready" companies planned to increase R&D spend by more than 10% in the year ahead with the aim of developing breakthrough innovations. The top 5 firms (Apple, Tesla, Amazon, Alphabet, Microsoft) employed a multifaceted approach to bolster their innovation capabilities. They actively sought out external knowledge and expertise, often through mergers and acquisitions, to augment their internal capabilities, competencies and resources. By strategically acquiring innovative technologies, processes, and talent, these companies rapidly accelerated their innovation efforts and made informed decisions that yielded maximum value from their investments. Equally, those firms who were not considered to be culturally orientated toward innovation faced the common barriers that often impede creativity, such as, siloed structures, a resistance to change, and inadequate resource allocation.[26]

A firm's culture significantly influences its capacity for innovation, shaping its strategic outlook, policies, investments, and human capital. A culture that embraces experimentation, risk-taking, and continuous learning is more likely to foster innovation and transform ideas into new or improved products, services, or processes. Conversely, a culture that is risk-averse and resistant to change will hinder the development of new and innovative ideas. Risk-taking is a critical element of corporate decision-making with decision makers evaluating alternatives that range from having a 'certain outcome' to 'taking a gamble'. The relationship between performance and risk-taking is complex and while some organizations may shy away from risk, others embrace it as a catalyst for growth. Firms with a history of chronic underperformance are more likely to be risk-averse due to their inability to effectively identify and capitalize on market opportunities. Paradoxically, some research indicates that low-performing organizations may also exhibit higher risk-taking (perhaps as a gamble) on moonshot projects to turnaround the firm. Conversely, high-performing businesses often demonstrate a greater willingness to take calculated risks which have subsequently produced higher-than-average industry performance.[27,28,29,30,31]

The CEO's Role in R&D: Driving Innovation and Shaping the Future

Investments in R&D are a cornerstone of success for firms, particularly in terms of driving innovation, competitive advantage, and improved market performance. As mentioned earlier, some firms are more 'culturally orientated' toward R&D investments than others, however, in broad terms, our understanding of a firm's R&D expenditure is primarily influenced by issues such as country norms, industry lifecycle stage, and corporate strategy.[32,33,34] The ability of an organization to innovate depends on access to knowledge, resources and capabilities to deliver successful R&D based outcomes in the form of new products and services, and central to this discussion is the role of the CEO. As the strategic leader of a firm, the CEO sets the organizational vision, drives investment decisions, and shapes the culture. Their leadership style can also significantly impact a firm's R&D orientation. Some CEOs are known to lead from the front with a top-down innovation agenda, whilst others create a bottom-up approach by developing an organizational culture that values innovation and embeds it into the DNA of the business through consistent investments in R&D. Either way, to be successful, a CEO needs to be committed to backing innovation-led growth strategies from both internal sources and external ecosystems.

However, whilst leadership style is important, a CEO's age is known to be the most significant predictor of R&D spending and innovation in organizations. Essentially, younger CEOs are generally better at perceiving and understanding emerging technologies and trends and are more willing to take risks and adopt more aggressive R&D investment strategies than their older CEO counterparts. In addition, though older CEOs have a wealth of industry experience, they are more inclined to reduce exposure to firm risk as they get older, and they are less likely to invest significant levels of R&D expenditure in innovation-based activities.[35,36] Interestingly, the previously mentioned Boston Consulting Group's survey of the world's 'Most Innovative Companies' in 2023 revealed that the average age of CEOs at the top five most innovative companies (Apple, Tesla, Amazon, Alphabet, Microsoft) was 53.4 years. In comparison, the average age of legacy media firms (Walt Disney Co., Paramount, Comcast, News Corp, AT&T) was older at 60.2 years. Additionally, the average age of CEOs at social media firms (X/Twitter, Snapchat, Pinterest, LinkedIn and TikTok) was just 32.8 years. Though this evidence is anecdotal, it supports the widely held belief that the more technologically focused social media firms are led by younger CEOs.

Arguably, older CEOs are less likely to be able to accurately assess the potential of unanticipated market opportunities and emerging technologies. This point was illustrated by longitudinal study that tracked 4,493 CEOs at U.S. firms between 1992 and 2010 which indicated that firms led by older CEOs were less likely to drive forward strategic initiatives like mergers and alliances.[37] Building on the argument that some CEOs are able to frame new market opportunities better than others, a plausible conclusion is that those with substantive career experience in sales and marketing or R&D are more market orientated and aim to drive revenue and competitive advantage by investing in R&D activities that can deliver new products and services. They also consider innovation as a market gamble worth taking, compared to generalist CEOs, with throughput experience in the form of general management, administration or finance, who may evaluate innovation through the lens of lower risk exposure and achieving a certain outcome from their R&D investments.

As mentioned earlier in Chapter 3: Diagnosing Corporate Trauma, R&D expenditure is an important metric that can provide valuable insights into a firm's performance, with sustained high spending demonstrating a commitment to innovation and developing new products and services, and improved operational efficiency. It is a metric that signals a focus on long-term success, rather than just short-term profits and indicates a firm's intention to remain relevant and adapt to future market changes. Moreover, a key physiological marker in diagnosing Corporate Trauma is 'R&D Intensity' which has been found to indicate that higher levels of R&D activity in relation to sales revenue is a good predictor of long-term corporate performance. Indeed, recent research examined the top 5 most innovative firms, as identified in the Boston Consulting Group's survey of the world's 'Most Innovative Companies' found that these firms had a R&D Intensity average of 12.6% over the period 2000–2023.[38] On an individual firm basis, the findings indicated average R&D Intensity figures for Tesla Inc. (25.90%), Microsoft (14.77%), Alphabet (13.63%) leading the way, followed by Amazon (8.90%) and Apple (4.70%). The fact that these leading firms compete in a range of different industries renders the argument for an 'industry norm' for R&D expenditure obsolete, whilst there is a strong argument for these firms being more 'culturally orientated' toward R&D as the key driver in delivering competitive advantage and improved market performance.

Are Newly Appointed CEOs Doomed to Fail?

Drawing inspiration from Epigenetics, we know that a severe environmental event can produce 'inherited transgenerational' physiological and psychological effects in organisms. The concept of Corporate Trauma argues that a corporate crisis can have lasting, negative consequences on an organization and that the inherited transgenerational responses are akin to numerous newly appointed CEOs trying to turnaround a failing business. Whilst each new CEO will attempt to significantly impact an organization's trajectory with a new set of corporate objectives and expectations[39,40,41] the longer-term consequences of the initial crisis seemed to be passed down through multiple generations of executive leadership.

Whilst literature establishes a link between CEO tenure and firm performance, there is also widespread agreement that the length of a CEO's tenure is finite. As mentioned previously, The Harvard Law School Forum on Corporate Governance has conducted extensive longitudinal research into CEO succession practices at U.S. public companies between 2000 and 2020.[42] Within the S&P 500, companies with poor financial performance, as measured by Total Shareholder Return, have historically not hesitated to replace their CEOs if they did not meet financial targets or were not providing a clear vision for the company's future in a way that engages employees and boosts investor confidence. Indeed, between 2017 and 2020, forced CEO departures in the S&P 500 due to underperformance amounted to 60% which suggests that financial performance remains a critical factor in determining the length of a CEO's tenure.

A key finding from The Harvard Law School Forum on Corporate Governance which underpins the argument for an inherited Corporate Trauma is the 'average tenure' of a CEO in the S&P 500. Recent years have witnessed fluctuations in the tenure of departing CEOs, driven by two opposing forces. On one hand, a buoyant stock market has encouraged longer leadership tenures; whilst on the other, an aging CEO population has necessitated leadership transitions. In 2020, the average tenure of departing CEOs in the S&P 500 was 9.3 years, up from the previous year and the longest since 2015. A CEO's tenure shorter than this figure is likely to indicate underlying executive performance issues.

As mentioned earlier in Chapter 3: Diagnosing Corporate Trauma, frequent CEO turnover is a key physiological marker of trauma where repeated leadership changes are a symptom of deeper, underlying issues within a company, rather than a solution to address chronic underperformance. The cases of Yahoo Inc. (2008), Nokia (2010) and WeWork (2019) are good examples of how a corporate crisis can destabilize leadership and result in rapid CEO turnover as each company sought to restore confidence, trust and credibility with stakeholders. Indeed, in the case of Yahoo Inc., a crisis in the form of a hostile bid from Microsoft Corporation resulted in six CEOs being appointed in just four years. The crisis subsequently triggered a downturn in corporate financial performance that successive CEO were unable to reverse using the classic turnaround playbook of changing strategy, restructuring operations and cost-cutting.[43]

Drawing on Epigenetics knowledge, we can consider CEO turnover as a manifestation of an inherited and transgenerational response to a crisis. When companies experience repeated failures, they often resort to a quick fix solution by replacing the CEO. This approach, however, can exacerbate the underlying problems rather than address them. There is no doubt that newly appointed CEOs often face the daunting task of revitalizing failing companies, and the allure of quick fixes in the form of restructuring and cost-cutting measures is understandable given the pressure to deliver immediate results. As such, new CEOs may prioritize visible and easily implemented solutions which whilst providing temporary relief, are unlikely to address the fundamental issues that are hindering the organization's long-term success. Indeed, they may have inherited a dysfunctional culture, a lack of trust, and a fear of failure, all of which creates a cycle of instability that hinders their capacity to implement effective changes and improve performance. As each new CEO comes in and fails to deliver sustainable results, the company's reputation suffers, its share price declines, and its employees become demoralized. This, in turn, can lead to further leadership turnover, perpetuating a vicious cycle of serial failed turnaround attempts. The classic turnaround playbook has been deployed several times, and yet, these efforts have proven to be futile, leaving the company trapped in a downward spiral. At some point, a newly appointed CEO has to ask an obvious question of its Board of Directors . . . what *'exactly'* is the problem? By recognizing the potential negative consequences of frequent CEO turnover, organizations can take steps to break this cycle by identifying the root cause of a firm's chronic ill health and underperformance.

In Chapter 5: Diagnosing Cases of Corporate Trauma, we will examine realworld case studies that illustrate how corporate crises have had a profound and transgenerational impact on each organization's leadership, culture and financial performance. The case studies offer a fresh lens to explain why some organizations cannot easily be turned around. Furthermore, we can identify a specific moment in time when a crisis event created an adaptive change in corporate culture and performance. Each case study will 'diagnose the root cause' of chronic corporate underperformance and the inherited cultural attitudes and behaviors that have combined to determine a traumatized firm's track record of serial failed turnaround.

Chapter 5
Diagnosing Cases of Corporate Trauma

Chronic corporate underperformance is a persistent challenge that plagues count-less organizations. Despite the best efforts of successive CEOs and strategic over-hauls, some companies remain trapped in a vicious cycle of under achievement. The beginning of the book prompted readers to take a *'leap of imagination'* in order to consider a new and innovative concept which argued that organizations can suffer from PTSD, triggered by a significant corporate crisis. The resulting trauma becomes deeply embedded in the culture of an organization and mani-fests as dysfunctional behaviors, negative attitudes, and a resistance to change. Over time, these effects can be inherited by subsequent generations of leadership, hindering even the most well-intentioned turnaround efforts. By drawing on in-sights from the emerging biological field of Epigenetics, the notion of Corporate Trauma argues that traumatic events can influence the expression of an organiza-tion's 'genetic' make-up. This novel approach provides an 'alternative diagnosis' for sustained corporate underachievement and offers a new lens through which to understand and address the root cause of chronic underperformance. Ulti-mately, by recognizing and addressing the hidden scars of Corporate Trauma, or-ganizations can break free from the cycle of serial failed turnaround attempts and embark on a path of recovery, sustainable growth and success.

The problem with taking 'a leap of imagination' in the context of Corporate Trauma is that it can lead to wild speculation and unsubstantiated claims. While the concept is intriguing and offers an innovative perspective, the following dis-cussion will argue the case for Corporate Trauma. It will present empirical evi-dence on a range of organizations that have experienced a corporate crisis in order to move the concept from something that is theoretically plausible, to an idea based on concrete evidence. The aphorism *'extraordinary claims require ex-traordinary evidence'* is a cornerstone of scientific inquiry as it emphasizes that the more extraordinary a claim is, the more compelling and rigorous the evidence supporting it must be. This principle encourages critical thinking and enables claims of the existence of Corporate Trauma to be based on rigorous evidence from reliable sources. As such, by approaching the topic with a balanced and evi-dence-based perspective, we can harness the potential of this original idea to bet-ter understand and address the challenges of serial failed turnaround attempts.

Typically, an analysis of between four and ten case studies has been found to provide a good basis on which to consider the validity and analytical generaliza-tion of empirical observations to theory.[1] As such, the following discussion will examine the crises of American International Group, Barclays PLC, BlackBerry,

https://doi.org/10.1515/9783111571126-005

BP, Wells Fargo & Co. and Volkswagen AG. Each of these companies and their crises will no doubt be familiar, perhaps considered as being consigned to history, or conceivably forgotten given that some of these events occurred over the course of the past two decades. However, each of these case studies will demonstrate the 'stress reaction' to a previous crisis and make explicit the impact of a hidden and inherited Corporate Trauma that continues to impede each company's ability to successfully revitalize and turnaround their fortunes.

The value in exploring Corporate Trauma using case studies is that they are considered an ideal research method to explore new ideas and theories, particularly, in the early stages of their development.[2,3] They also tend to focus on real-world business and management issues that can provide powerful insights into organizational dynamics and deliver relevant and actionable knowledge for practitioners.[4,5] Each case study follows the same protocol and provides a clear and triangulated chain of evidence, from different sources of data, that will provide readers with a reliable platform on which to take that leap of imagination and a mental jump into the world of Corporate Trauma.

In diagnosing Corporate Trauma each case study will provide: a brief overview of the company's history; details of the Critical Corporate Incident and the precise date (e.g. the World Trade Centre attacks on September 11th 2001) that triggered the downturn in performance; the adaptive changes in cultural attitudes and behaviors toward innovation and risk; the short-term effects and the long-term consequences on corporate culture and financial performance; and the recurrent changes in CEO leadership. A concise and readily accessible quick reference guide in Appendix 2 (Corporate Trauma: case study matrix) provides a consolidated overview of the key markers of Corporate Trauma which will help readers to navigate through each case study and quickly locate the critical data.

As mentioned previously in Chapter 3: Diagnosing Corporate Trauma, the development of metrics to diagnose the trauma were, in particular, informed by the studies of the inherited transgenerational effects of PTSD in babies of mothers exposed to the World Trade Center attacks during pregnancy.[6,7] Whilst mothers suffered enduring psychological changes in the form of PTSD, depression and anxiety, their babies suffered from physiological effects in the form of a significantly 'lower' than average birth weight and size. Just as individuals may carry the scars of personal trauma for generations, so too can organizations bear the burden of Corporate Trauma. Understanding the long-term consequences of such events is crucial for developing effective strategies to mitigate their impact and foster greater organizational resilience. Importantly, each case study compares the data for each organization 'before and after' the corporate crisis to identify the significant changes in each of the physiological (e.g. financial decline) and psychological (e.g. a risk averse culture) markers of Corporate Trauma. As you will see, as with the babies who were born to mothers of the 9/11 attacks, each case study provides evidence which strongly suggests that a significant corporate crisis has resulted in profound and long-lasting consequences. The damage extends beyond immediate financial penalties and reputational harm, with fundamental shifts in corporate culture and investor perception which has hindered long-term recovery and resulted in a company that is 'smaller' and 'less healthy' over multiple generations of the organization. The classic turnaround playbook has proved insufficient to overcome a deep-seated trauma that has become ingrained in each company, despite numerous attempts to improve performance by successive CEOs. After reading the case studies you should ask yourself the following questions: would the appointment of a new CEO improve each company's performance?; assuming that a new CEO will deploy a classic turnaround playbook . . . will it work?

AIG: Doing what it Does Best . . . but Fraudulently!

Background

With a market capitalization of over US$45 billion and an annual revenue of over US$27 billion in 2024, the American International Group Inc. (AIG) is a company of immense size and stature. These numbers are, however, dwarfed by a comparison to figures from before the corporate crisis which occurred in 2005. A market capitalization of over US$144 billion and revenues of almost US$98 billion in 2004 had made AIG a global insurance colossus that dominated in both its domestic and international markets.

AIG was founded by Cornelius Vander Starr in 1919, in Shanghai, China. Originally established as the American Asiatic Underwriters insurance agency, these humble beginnings marked the start of a journey that would see the company become one of the world's largest insurance and financial services companies. Furthermore, there is a strong argument to suggest that AIG's development, growth and success in its early years can be attributed to its founder's visionary leadership and entrepreneurial spirit, which was instrumental in establishing a corporate culture that valued innovation, risk management, and customer service. Over the years, AIG's diversified business model encompassed various insurance products and services which helped mitigate risks and ensure financial stability during numerous economic downturns. It also enabled the company to develop and expand into international markets and capitalize on the emerging opportunities presented after World War II in terms of satisfying an increasing consumer need for insurance coverage. Today, AIG is a global property, casualty and specialty insurance company with a presence in 190 countries, and operates in three market segments: General Insurance, Life and Retirement, and Other Operations (the company's institutional asset management business).

The development of AIG has not been without its challenges, the most momentous being the significant difficulties it faced during the Global Financial Crisis (2007–2009) and its exposure to the U.S. subprime mortgage market. The collapse of this market triggered a chain reaction, affecting many financial institutions around the world which led to a severe global economic crisis. AIG was deemed 'too big to fail' by policymakers and economists, as its collapse would have caused a series of events leading to the bankruptcy of other financial institutions in an already destabilized global economy. The Federal Reserve Bank of New York provided AIG with an initial US$85 billion of financial support in September 2008 in return for a 79.9% ownership stake in the company with a trust established for the sole benefit of the U.S. Department of the Treasury. With a total package of support amounting to US$182 billion, the AIG bailout remains one of the largest government interventions in U.S. history. In December 2012, its shares were returned to public ownership and resulted in a profit for the Federal Reserve and Treasury that amounted to US$22.7 billon.[1]

A Corporate Crisis: The Trigger that Caused a Downward Spiral

In early 2005, the New York State Attorney General, the New York Insurance Department and the U.S. Securities and Exchange Commission collectively began their investigation into a series of allegedly fraudulent financial transactions by AIG and its senior executives.

AIG's Critical Corporate Incident (CCI) occurred on 2nd February 2005 with investigators filing charges against the company for accounting fraud and bid rigging. The core accusation centered on AIG's practice of booking loans as revenue, a deceptive maneuver designed to artificially inflate the company's share price. Furthermore, the U.S. Securities and Exchange Commission stated that long serving Chairman of the Board of Directors and CEO, Maurice Greenberg, and Chief Financial Officer, Howard Smith, along with 20 other senior executives were aware of and "recklessly disregarded" AIG's fraudulent financial transactions over the period of "at least 2000 until 2005"[2,3] in order to create an artificial impression, that under their leadership, the company had consistently delivered double-digit growth in key financial performance metrics. On one occasion, a press release from Greenburg commented on AIG's fourth quarter earnings in 2000 which had been "a very good quarter and year. We added US$106 million to AIG's general insurance net loss and loss adjustment reserves for the quarter".[3] The financial markets reacted positively to the news with one analyst saying that

AIG was "doing what it does best: growing fast and making the numbers".[3] In reality, there had been a US$144 million decrease in reserves.[4]

Greenburg and Smith's intentional wrongdoing and fraudulent behavior concealed the fact that AIG had encountered a series of financial difficulties that, had they been duly reported and accounted for, would have exposed substantial operational shortcomings and prevented the company from achieving certain earnings and growth benchmarks. Secondary charges were filed against AIG which included accusations of violations relating to: concealing underwriting losses by converting them into capital losses; misleading the New York Insurance Department about its offshore affiliates; and improper reporting of workers' compensation premiums. This fraudulent activity, over at least a five-year period, was estimated to have cost investors US$3.5 billion.

On the 26th May 2005, Greenburg and Smith were sued, and by the 9th February 2006 AIG was fined a total of US$1.64 billion. Of which, US$800 million would go to investors deceived by false financial statements, US$375 million to AIG policyholders harmed by bid rigging activities, and US$344 million to U.S. states involved with workers' compensation funds. Additionally, a US$100 million fine was to be paid to the State of New York and US$25 million in connection with the Department of Justice.[4]

This Critical Corporate Incident resulted in significant short-term effects and longer-term consequences for AIG. In the immediate aftermath, Greenburg was fired after 38 years as the CEO of AIG, as was Howard Smith. Whilst the company regretted and apologized for its behavior, the damage to its reputation was significant, particularly amongst investors with share prices dropping by 9% in one week and 24% in 8 weeks.

Fast forward to 2024 and some AIG executives may be applauding the company's 17% share price increase over the previous 12 months. This recent performance, however, hides a hidden trauma where the long-term decline in share price can be traced back to the date of the CCI. Benchmarked against 'best-in-class' companies, AIG's share price had outperformed against these firms in 2004, however, since the 2nd February 2005 its share price has collapsed, falling 94% compared to firms in the S&P Global 1200 Index which have increased in value by 220%.[5] Moreover, the share price has flatlined since September 2008 when the U.S. Government commenced its majority ownership. However, this holding was fully divested in 2012 with AIG taking back full control of its business. It is reasonable to assume that the day-to-day running of AIG would have been subject to some political interference, an increase in bureaucratic procedures, and an operating model that led to inefficiencies in decision-making and resource allocation. It was no surprise, therefore, that the company's lackluster share price performance during this four-year period would have diminished investor confidence and belief in the company's future prospects. However, a "new" company had

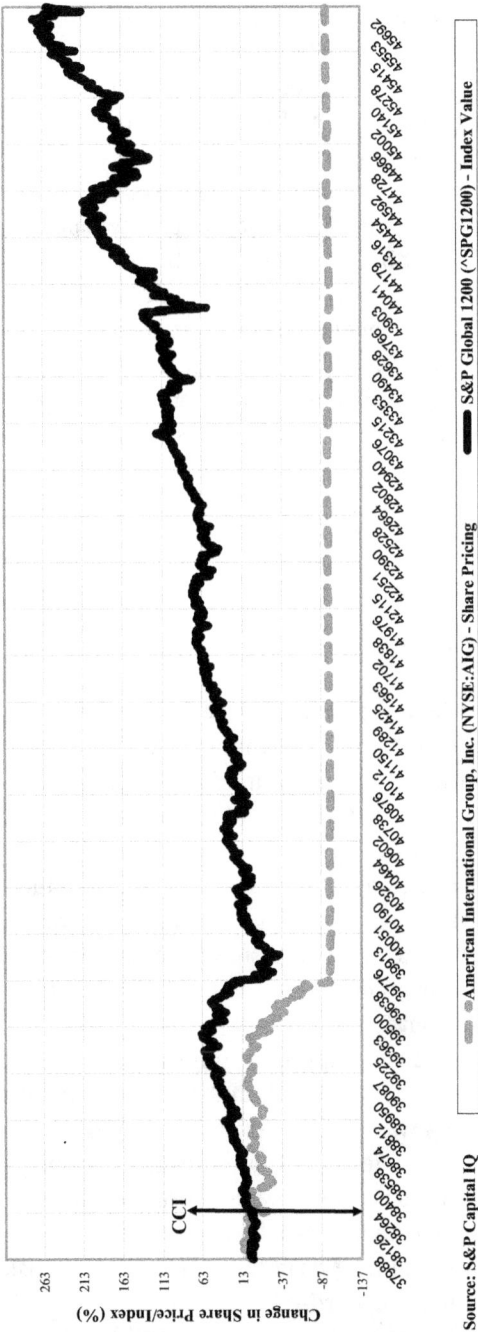

Diagram 1: Share Price Performance of AIG v S&P Global 1200 Index (2004–2025).

Source: S&P Capital IQ

emerged in 2013 with AIG realigned, refocused and "ready to take on and meet the challenges of building a better future".[6] The new strategy aimed to attract investors and improve the company's credit rating by focusing on cost-cutting, better risk management, and more efficient operational processes. However, the share price of the newly reborn AIG, when compared with best-in-class competitors on the S&P Global 1200 Index, indicates a continued period of stagnation (see Diagram 1). It suggests that the company has failed to capitalize on new opportunities, innovate, and deliver consistent growth. Furthermore, AIGs Total Debt levels decreased substantially, from US$201,344 million in 2008 to US$9,790 million in 2024, and whilst this has resulted in a stronger balance sheet, the company's debt reduction may have been prioritized over investment in innovative new products and services, potentially slowing growth and future returns for investors. When viewed through the lens of Corporate Trauma, AIGs dormant share price is indicative of a stress reaction to the CCI that has left the company, in the estimation of investors, with a chronic illness that has significantly impacted on its reputation and financial performance.

An Adverse Modification in Corporate Culture

Corporate culture is often regarded as intangible and illusive when it comes to measuring a company's cultural dynamics. Corporate Trauma proposes a more focused approach, examining the critical psychological marker of cultural attitudes to 'innovation' and 'risk-taking' which are fundamental to long-term growth and competitiveness. Companies that prioritize innovation, often through substantial R&D investments, are more likely to develop groundbreaking products and services. However, a crisis can dramatically disrupt innovation-led growth strategies as organizations shift their focus to immediate survival and reputation management. As such, investments in innovation may be curtailed, and risk aversion may become the prevailing mindset, but for how long?

Diagram 2 below illustrates a frequency analysis of innovation and risk words in annual reports over the period 2000 and 2024. In 2000, the frequency gap between innovation and risk words was clearly pronounced, and as one might expect from a financial company, attitudes to risk far outweighed attitudes to innovation. By 2005, AIG had become less risk averse and more innovative in their outlook. However, since the CCI the company has become culturally more risk averse, as indicated by the upward and long-term trend in the use of risk words compared to the use of innovation-based words.

The long-term consequences of the CCI have been far-reaching. Risk aversion appears to have increased over the long-term, which has most likely discouraged the already minimal R&D investment activities and hindered corporate growth. The lack of investor confidence mentioned above, leading to a decline in market capitalization, may have restricted access to capital, and an ability to fund innovative projects. Regrettably, AIG does not explicitly report R&D expenditure in its financial statements and so the crucial physiological marker of innovation, R&D Intensity, cannot be determined.

AIG

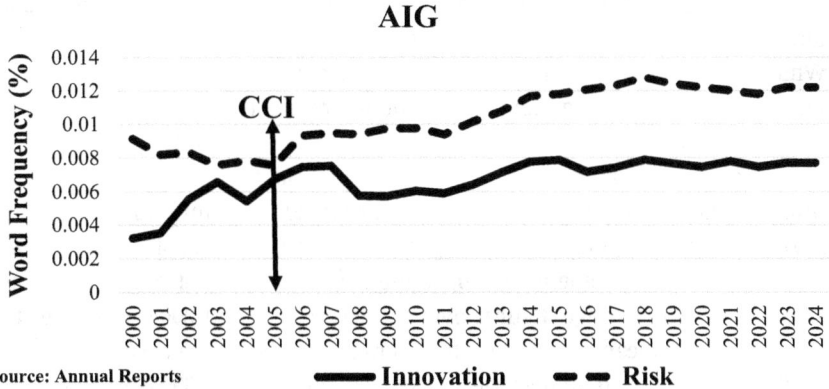

Diagram 2: Cultural Attitudes to Innovation and Risk (2000–2024).

Corporate Financial Performance

AIG entered the new millennium with impressive financial results. A market capitalization of US$193,532 million was backed up with revenues of US$56,338 million and an operating income of US$13,806 million for the financial year 2000. By 2024, the financial picture had drastically changed for the worse with market capitalization at US$45,331 million, revenues falling to US$27,027 million, whilst operating income had declined to US$4,228 million. Like babies born to mothers of the 9/11 attacks, AIG is now a much smaller company following the crisis.

While AIG had been a global insurance giant for decades, the period between 2000 and 2004 was marked by significant financial challenges including a series of losses related to the 9/11 attacks and the bursting of the Dot.com bubble. As we can see from the previous discussion on cultural attitudes to innovation and risk, AIG adopted more aggressive risk-taking practices between 2000 and 2004 and wrongly engaged in deceptive and fraudulent accounting practices. The seeds of the company's future problems had been sown.

The company's history of aggressive risk-taking saw its financial products division engage in high-risk, high-reward strategies and when the housing market collapsed, millions of subprime mortgage holders began to default on their loans. AIG's market capitalization catastrophically disintegrated from US$126,495 million in 2007 to just US$1,130 million a year later. The company's operating income also dramatically plummeted from US$15,477 million in 2007 to a loss of US$12,534 million in 2008. AIG were on the brink of collapse. Unable to access capital to meet its financial obligations caused a severe liquidity crunch which resulted in a government bailout and one of the most prominent casualties of the Global Financial Crisis.

While the review of AIG's financial performance describes a company facing an existential crisis, the core argument for Corporate Trauma is that the CCI on 2nd February 2005 had triggered a downward spiral. Table 1 below illustrates the key physiological markers of the trauma by comparing the financial performance from 'before and after' the CCI. As such, the financial results for 2005 are an important benchmark. With a market capitalization of US$179,815 million, revenue of US$108,781 million and an operating income of US$20,913 million, AIGs financial results are better than the equivalent 'average' figures over the years 2000 and 2004. However, the 2005 results are significantly less than the 'average' figures for the ensuing years between 2006 and 2024 with an average market capitalization US$59,311 million; average revenues of US$58,865 million; and an average operating income of US$6,510 million. Perhaps the most significant evidence of Corporate Trauma's impact on the company's financial health lies in the 'Change in Post CCI Average since 2005'. This analysis reveals alarming figures: a 67% reduction in market capitalization, a 46% decline in revenue, and a severe drop in operating income of 69%. This substantial downturn in financial results strongly indicates deep-seated issues affecting the company's strategic direction and how efficiently it operates.

Table 1: AIG Comparative Average Financial Performance (2000–2024).

Source: S&P Capital IQ	Pre-CCI Average (2000–2004)	Critical Corporate Incident (2005)	Post-CCI Average (2006–2024)	Change in Post CCI Average since 2005 (%)
Market Capitalization (US$ mn)	166,976	179,815	59,311	−67
Revenue (US$ mn)	72,430	108,781	58,865	−46
Operating Income (US$ mn)	15,042	20,913	6,510	−69

A Transgenerational Response Over Multiple Corporate Generations

Frequent CEO turnover is a symptom of deeper corporate issues where the trauma of a corporate crisis is inherited from one senior executive to another. AIG have experienced repeated failures and resorted to quick-fix solutions like CEO replacements, which has exacerbated the company's underlying problems leading to a cycle of organizational instability and serial failed turnarounds.

To illustrate this point, Maurice Greenburg led AIG for nearly four decades as the CEO. Between 1968 and 2005 he turned the company from a relatively small insurance firm into a global financial powerhouse. Greenberg's autocratic leadership style and aggressive approach to business strategy propelled AIGs expansion into numerous countries and diversified its product offerings. However, this aggressive strategy also led to an increased appetite for risk-taking, and as we have seen in Diagram 2 above, particularly during the period 2000 to 2005.

The CCI on the 2nd February 2005, marked a significant turning point for AIG. It resulted in the short-term effects of Greenburg's resignation, a significant drop in AIGs share price, and a government bailout of historic proportions. The longer-term consequences of this crisis include a cultural adaption in the company's attitudes to innovation and risk, a tarnished reputation, and chronic financial underperformance. AIG had become a 'classic' turnaround case. However, the evidence presented above indicates that the trauma of the crisis, and serial failed turnarounds, has been inherited by numerous CEOs.

Enter, Martin J. Sullivan who was appointed CEO in March 2005. Sullivan's appointment was a response by AIG's Board of Directors to the mounting regulatory pressure and investigations surrounding the company's accounting practices and business dealings. He joined AIG in 1971 and held various management positions throughout his 37-year career with the company and was widely regarded as a safe pair of hands to address the company's governance issues and implement reforms that would restore public and shareholder confidence. During his tenure, between 2005 and 2008, Sullivan addressed the challenges faced by AIG in the wake of the financial scandal and took a number of actions to improve transparency, strengthen corporate governance, and establish best practices. Sullivan stated that AIG had made "major advances in our corporate governance and management practices" and had "conducted an extensive internal review of our accounting and reporting policies and procedures".[7] He also set a positive new strategic direction that focused on driving down costs, improving operational processes and a growth strategy that expanded the company's presence in emerging international markets. However, Sullivan's optimism stood in stark contrast to the financial performance of AIG during his tenure. The company experienced a significant decline in multiple key financial metrics, with its market capitalization catastrophically collapsing from US$179,815 million to just US$1,130 million between 2005 and 2008. Furthermore, revenue fell from US$108,781 million to US$63,871 million over the same period, whilst operating income fell from US$20,913 million in 2005 to a substantial operating loss of U$12,534 million in 2008. This severe deterioration in the company's profitability and operational efficiency over the three-year period of Sullivan's tenure is a clear indication of not only chronic levels of corporate under-performance, but near ruinous levels of financial losses. Sullivan's term as CEO lasted just three years and ended with the company on the brink of collapse.

Next up, Robert B. Willumstad, who assumed the role of Chairman and CEO of AIG on the 15th June 2008. As an experienced financial services executive, he had previously been appointed to AIGs Board of Directors in 2006, however, his tenure as CEO was short lived. Unable to implement his strategy due to the emerging consequences of the U.S. housing market crash, AIG's reliance on mort-gage-backed securities plunged the company into a devastating cash crisis at a time when well-known financial institutions such as Bear Stearns and Lehman Brothers had collapsed. Willumstad stepped down as CEO on the 16th September 2008 after just three months in charge.

On 18th September 2008, Edward M. Liddy was appointed as interim Chair-man and CEO at the request of the U.S. government who provided an emergency US$85 billion loan in return for a majority equity stake in AIG. Liddy inherited an organization that was "stunned and bewildered" and a "shambles".[8] Liddy's plan emphasized the need to stabilize the company and focus on its core insurance business and avoid excessive risk-taking. Furthermore, the company would repay the loan by selling off many of its major global businesses and as the global eco-nomic crisis deepened, potential buyers of AIG assets had difficulty securing enough financing to complete deals. Liddy's tenure as CEO lasted 11 months until he stepped down in August 2009.

Robert H. Benmosche, a highly respected executive was appointed CEO on 10th August 2009 due to his extensive experience of restructuring complex finan-cial organizations. During Benmosche's tenure the company embarked on a sig-nificant restructuring plan, including asset sales and divestitures, to strengthen its balance sheet, reduce debt and create value. The strategic focus shifted to-wards simplifying the core insurance business by divesting assets and rebuilding trust in what was considered to be a toxic brand. Benmosche's tenure as CEO re-flects a company in transition. The focus was on stabilizing the business, reducing costs and debt, rebuilding its reputation, improving credit ratings and laying the groundwork for a sustainable future. By 2012, Benmoshe had overseen three years of full-year profits, and importantly, AIG had fully repaid the US$182 billion of financial support from the U.S. government, plus a profit. Benmoshe had suc-cessfully stabilized the company and had returned it to private ownership during his five years leading the firm. Investor sentiment had returned with a 335% increase in market capitalization, supplemented by an operating profit that had increased by 259%, although revenue had decreased by 12%. On the face of it the classic turnaround playbook had worked.

Peter D. Hancock was appointed CEO on 1st September, 2014 after leading AIGs property-casualty business since March 2011. The focus of his tenure aimed to prioritize core insurance businesses in a way that "balanced a mix of growth, profitability, and risk"[9] by simplifying the business model, streamlining operations, and reducing debt whilst growing core businesses in home and international markets. Hancock's tenure as CEO essentially aimed to simplify AIGs business by moving it from being a complex conglomerate to a more streamlined and focused organization with centralized leadership. However, the financial metrics paint a stark picture of a company in significant distress. A decline in market capitalization, revenue, and operating profit over a three-year period signaled a severe deterioration in the company's financial health. Market capitalization decreased by 17%, with the loss of investor confidence and concerns about AIGs future earnings potential and a 19% decrease in revenue indicated a contraction in the company's core business operations. The most alarming metric was the 98% decline in operating profit. In March 2017, Hancock announced his intention to resign after the company had posted a fourth quarter loss of US$3 billion in 2016. He stepped down after just three years, commenting that he did not have "wholehearted shareholder support for my continued leadership".[10] A repetitive pattern of serial failed turnaround attempts had started to emerge with each successive CEO inheriting the effects of a hidden corporate trauma that had consistently undermined AIGs health, development and performance.

Brian Duperreault was appointed as CEO on the 14th May 2017. As a highly experienced executive in insurance with a previous 23-year career with AIG, his introduction to investors and employees praised his abilities as an 'innovation champion' who had a proven track record of driving business growth and financial performance by delivering 'innovative client solutions'. Duperreault's tenure was characterized by a commitment to transform AIG into a more efficient, profitable, and customer-centric organization that would restore its position as a leading global insurance company. Successfully implementing cost-cutting and efficiency strategies would improve the financial stability of the company, its credit rating and reorient it towards sustainable profitability and growth. In 2018, Duperreault commented that AIG was "emerging from more than a decade of significant changes in leadership and shifting strategies" and that a strategic review of the company had revealed a number of legacy liabilities and "many issues and challenges that were deeper and more pervasive than we anticipated".[11] Over the course of his three-year tenure, Duperreault delivered on his commitment to improve AIGs profitability with cost-cutting and efficiency measures that increased operating income from US$2,902 million in 2017 to US$6,600 million in 2019. However, over the same period, revenues had flatlined and market capitalization was down by 21%. Duperreault had been appointed to streamline AIG and there is no doubt that he was successful in terms of improving profitability, but investors remained unconvinced about the turnaround.

Peter S. Zaffino, took over as CEO on the 1st January 2020 having previously held a number of senior executive roles that included his successful leadership of the transformation program AIG 200. On his appointment Zaffino commented that he was looking forward to the challenge of making the company "the leading insurance company in the world known for its strategic value, operational excellence and strong financial performance".[12] His transformation plan followed the classic turnaround playbook used by previous AIG CEOs (Benmoshe, Hancock, Duperreault) with key strategic themes focusing on improving financial performance, operational efficiency and focusing on core business. Zaffino's turnaround strategy, however, also included an emphasis on delivering long-term value to shareholders by returning billions of dollars through common stock repurchases and dividends. It is, therefore, no surprise to note that AIG's market capitalization has increased during Zaffino's tenure, from US$36,823 million in 2020 to US$45,331 million in 2024. Zaffino's approach has also focused on driving underwriting excellence, modernizing and streamlining operating infrastructure and enhancing digital effectiveness which has delivered significant cost-savings and helped to increase operating income from US$2,737 million to US$ 4,228 million between 2020 and 2024. Of great concern, however, is the four-year decline in revenue which deteriorated by 38%, from US$43,337 million to US$27,027 million over the same period. While the economic downturn caused by the COVID-19 pandemic, geopolitical tensions and economic volatility may partially explain the revenue decrease, the company's internal culture regarding innovation and risk points to a significant failure in developing high-quality, novel offerings that are competitive in the market. This lack of innovation likely fueled customer dissatisfaction and reduced sales.

Interestingly, in 2023 Zaffino stated that AIG had reclaimed a seat at the highest level of business and was "recognized as a leading global insurer"[13] and in 2024 he advised shareholders that the company had completed a multi-year transformation and a "remarkable turnaround" that had "produced outstanding financial results"[14] derived from underwriting discipline, divesting non-core businesses, reducing debt, and focusing on core business. However, in the context of Corporate Trauma, the jury is still out on the successful turnaround of AIG, particularly when considering the key physiological markers from 'before and after' the CCI in 2005 which indicate a substantial downturn in corporate financial performance.

In summary, Maurice Greenberg's 37-year stewardship of AIG fostered a period of remarkable organizational stability and sustained growth. However, the corporate crisis of 2005, which culminated in his departure, precipitated a significant and persistent decline in the company's performance. Despite numerous attempts, subsequent leadership has struggled to reverse this downward trajectory. The company has witnessed an unusually high rate of CEO turnover, with seven individuals occupying the position since 2005. This rapid succession of leaders has resulted in an average tenure of just 2.71 years, a stark contrast to the average of 9.3 years for CEOs within the S&P 500. This disparity underscores the profound challenges AIG has faced and the trauma that each CEO has inherited during their tenure.

Conclusion

Under the leadership of Peter Zaffino, AIG has made significant progress in improving its financial performance and operational efficiency. The classic turn-around playbook of focusing on core businesses, reducing debt, and implementing cost-cutting measures has improved the profitability of AIG. However, the recent upturn in AIGs fortunes when viewed through the lens of Corporate Trauma, indicates that the company had suffered a stress reaction to the crisis in 2005 which has created a number of dysfunctional adaptive physiological and psychological changes that have had a lasting impact on AIG's reputation, financial performance, and strategic direction. The evidence presented above provides the underpinning for a number of conclusions that support the notion of Corporate Trauma.

Firstly, the physiological financial markers demonstrate that there has been a significant decline in market capitalization, which can be pinpointed to the CCI on 2nd February 2005. Whilst the company made strides in recovering from the immediate crisis, its long-term share price performance has consistently under-performed when compared to best-in-class benchmarks. The impact on AIG's reputation has eroded investor confidence, which in turn may have made it more difficult for the company to access capital, further limiting its ability to fund growth initiatives. Furthermore, AIG's financial performance has experienced a significant decline since CCI of 2005. There is no doubt that the company faced a catastrophic challenge during the Global Financial Crisis, but the CCI triggered the initial downward spiral and a deep-seated trauma that is making it difficult to turnaround. The company's financial performance has been further impacted by increased costs and decreased revenue, likely due to a combination of factors such as regulatory costs, litigation expenses, and a decline in sales. However, the trauma of the CCI and its impact on AIG's financial health is most evident in the comparison of financial metrics from before and after the crisis event. In essence, AIG is a much smaller company now than before the crisis.

Secondly, the CCI of 2005 created an adaptive psychological change and lasting impact on AIG's culture. The crisis led to a marked increase in risk aversion and a decrease in innovative thinking, which is likely to have hindered the company's ability to invest in R&D and pursue innovative projects. Furthermore, AIG's lack of explicit reporting on R&D expenditure also makes it difficult to assess the true extent of its commitment to innovation and its ability to recover from the cultural impact of the CCI.

Thirdly, a succession of CEOs have attempted to turnaround AIG with the classic playbook of deploying strategies that include cost-cutting, restructuring, asset sales, and re-focusing the company on core business. However, many of these efforts have been unsuccessful as each CEO has inherited the lingering effects of a trauma that has created a number of adaptive changes that include: a damaged corporate reputation, a lack of investor confidence, an organizational culture that has become more risk averse, and chronic financial underperformance. It is no wonder that the average CEO tenure after the crisis event has been significantly less than the average CEO tenure across the S&P500 and the company's continued struggles indicate that AIG needs more than the classic turnaround playbook to reverse its fortunes.

Despite a 'new' AIG emerging in 2013 with a focus on cost-cutting and risk management, the company continues to stagnate. AIG's dormant share price, weak financial performance and multiple turnaround attempts reflects a long-term Corporate Trauma resulting from a scandal two decades ago. The scars left from the company's intentional fraud have been deep and enduring.

Barclays: If you ain't Cheating, you ain't Trying

Background

Founded in 1690 by goldsmith bankers John Freame and Thomas Gould in London, Barclays PLC (Barclays) boasts a rich history. In 1736, Joseph Freame, son of the founding partner, brought his brother-in-law James Barclay into the business, establishing the enduring name. Barclays has weathered centuries of change, numerous financial crises, global conflicts, and the transformative shifts of industrial and technological revolutions which is a testament to its continuing resilience.

Today, Barclays is a major player in the global financial services industry and operates in over 40 countries in Europe, the Americas, Africa, the Middle East, and Asia. Its diversified business model and strong brand recognition enables it to compete effectively, and mitigate risk, in a range of financial services markets that include retail banking, credit cards, wholesale banking, investment banking, wealth management, investment management services and securities dealing. At the end of the financial year 2024, Barclays market capitalization was over £42 billion, with revenue exceeding £24 billion and an operating income of more than £8 billion. At face value, Barclays would appear to be in healthy financial shape and its global reach suggests that the company is well positioned for continued growth and success in serving its 48 million customers and clients.

Barclays has faced several major difficulties over the years, the most prominent being the Global Financial Crisis. Unlike AIG, Barclays avoided a government bailout by embarking on a capital raising strategy which sought emergency funding from investors, including an initial £4.5 billion investment from the Qatar Investment Authority, and an additional £7.3 billion from various other investors. The circumstances surrounding these dealings later became a subject of controversy and a subsequent investigation by the UKs Financial Conduct Authority (FCA) revealed that Barclays recapitalization strategy had been "reckless and lacked integrity"[1] in terms of misleading shareholders and withholding vital information about the Qatari investment. Barclays was subsequently fined £40 million by the FCA.

Fast forward to 2024, and on 20th February, CEO C.S.Venkatakrishnan outlined his vision for Barclays to be a UK-centered leader in global finance by creating a simpler and less complex organization that would deliver better customer experiences, improved profitability and a more 'balanced' approach in terms of capital allocation by business and geographic scope. He stated that the launch of a new three-year strategy would improve the company's operational and financial performance and deliver a "best-in-class customer and client experience"[2] which would produce higher quality income growth and return billions of pounds to shareholders.

A Corporate Crisis: The Trigger that Caused a Downward Spiral

Barclays Critical Corporate Incident (CCI) occurred on the 27th June 2012 when the company was handed the largest fine in UK banking history for its fraudulent and anticompetitive behavior. The company was found guilty of consistently manipulating UK London Interbank Offered Rate (LIBOR) and the Euro Interbank Offered Rate (EURIBOR) benchmark interest rates which were used to calculate trillions of dollars' worth of financial contracts and derivatives between 2005 and 2012.[3] The fraud involved a significant number of employees whose intentionally deceptive behavior aimed to boost Barclays profits. This was particularly important during the Global Financial Crisis as it gave the false impression to stakeholders and the media that the company had ridden out the severe effects of the liquidity crisis.

A significant cross-border investigation between the Financial Services Authority in the UK, the U.S. Commodity Futures Trading Commission, the U.S. Department of Justice, the Federal Bureau of Investigation and the Securities and Exchange Commission resulted in Barclays being fined £284.4m as part of a £3.9bn settlement. UK and US regulators found that the company had 'intentionally' engaged in the deceptive and fraudulent manipulation of benchmark interest rates over many years. The damage to Barclays corporate reputation was considerable and CEO Bob Diamond resigned with George Osbourne, Chancellor of the Exchequer, saying that his departure was the "first step towards a new culture of responsibility"[4] in banking. The ramifications of the scandal continued into 2016, with Barclays being fined a further US$100m to settle with 44 US states where government and not-for profit agencies had suffered financial losses as a result of the fraud.

Barclays share price briefly recovered during 2013, with investor confidence boosted by new executive leadership and a successful rights issue which raised £5.8 billion in order to meet regulatory capital requirements. Furthermore, whilst operating income declined 34% between 2013 and 2015, progress had been made in cost-cutting initiatives which no doubt positively influenced investor sentiment, particularly at a time when the global economy was showing signs of recovery. However, since 2014 the long-term drift in Barclays share price indicates a hidden trauma that can be traced back to the date of the CCI. Diagram 3 below shows Barclay's share price had outperformed 'best-in-class' companies in the first quarter of 2012 but has drifted since with its share price increasing 64% at a time when the share price of firms in the S&P Global 1200 Index has increased 204%.[5] Furthermore, whilst Barclays share price has surged by a spectacular 76% over the past 12 months with market sentiment attracted by dividend payouts and the company's new 'Simpler, Better and More balanced' strategy, from a Corporate Trauma perspective, Barclays sluggish long-term share price performance, when compared with a broad measure of global stock market performance, reflects the lingering consequences of a stress reaction triggered by the CCI.

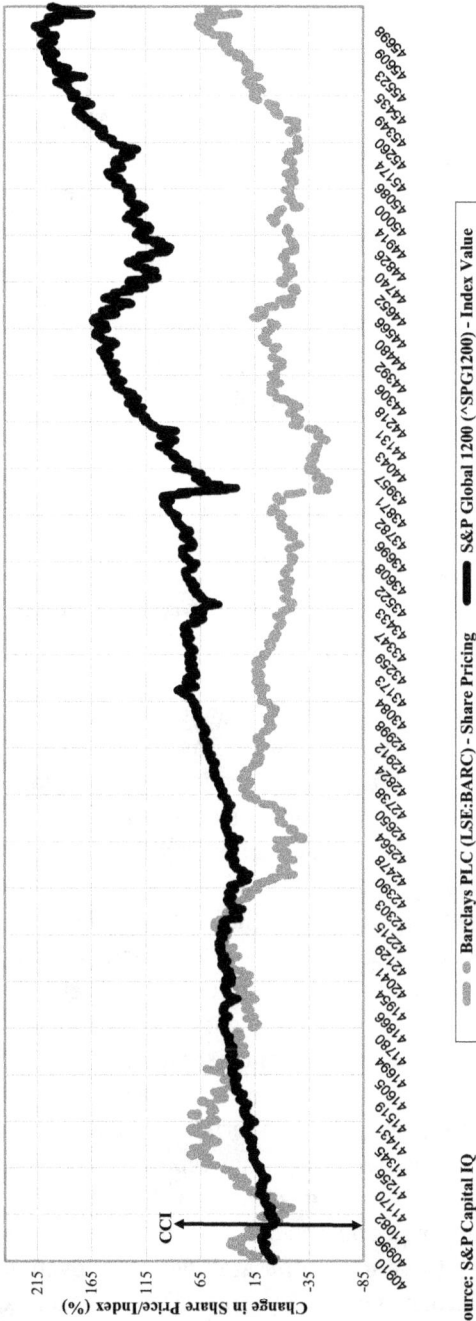

Source: S&P Capital IQ

Diagram 3: Share Price Performance of Barclays v S&P Global 1200 Index (2012–2025).

An Adverse Modification in Corporate Culture

"If you aint cheating, you aint trying"[6] remarked a Barclays Vice-President in 2010 when discussing a foreign exchange trade with one of his sales team. This comment was just one example The New York State Department of Financial Services found in its investigation into the manipulation of benchmark interest rates. Not only did some of Barclays managers intentionally encourage deceptive and fraudulent behavior, they also regularly gave presentations to new employees to explain how to manipulate interest rates as a part of their onboarding process.[6] Both UK and US authorities were critical of Barclays lack of internal controls and allowing a culture of misconduct to exist at different levels of employees, with little in the way of appropriate supervision or intervention by managers to address the fraudulent activities of its traders. This type of corporate behavior gives rise to many questions, but most importantly about the culture that existed at Barclays at the time. In the aftermath of the Global Financial Crisis, KPMG[7] reported that many financial firms' corporate culture was dominated by excessive risk taking, stimulated by short term incentive and remuneration policies. As such, Barclays were not an exceptional case when it came to the issue of corporate greed, deception and the fraudulent behavior of its employees.

The CCI triggered an adaptive change in Barclays culture in the wake of its corporate culpability and fines, in so far as, it embedded a new set of conduct and citizenship values in an attempt to guide it through a transformative phase of organizational development and improve investor confidence in a severely damaged corporate reputation. It introduced new governance structures and policies in 2013 as an important part of changing the culture and rebuilding trust by introducing: a Board Conduct, Reputation and Operational Risk Committee; mandatory training for all staff on the new Purpose (Helping people achieve their ambitions – in the right way) and Values (Respect, Integrity, Service, Excellence and Stewardship) of the organization; an annually assessed Code of Conduct; remuneration structures changed to identify 'how' results are delivered; and sales commission being replaced with performance measured against customer service metrics.

The idea of Corporate Trauma argues that a company's response to a crisis significantly impacts its long-term success, particularly in terms of its cultural attitudes towards innovation and risk-taking. Barclays do not report R&D investment spend in its annual reports but we are able to quantify how the CCI has impacted on its attitude to innovation and risk and whether or not the crisis has resulted in an adaptive psychological change in cultural attitudes to innovation and risk. Diagram 4 below illustrates a frequency analysis of innovation and risk words in annual reports over the period 2000 and 2024. In 2000, the frequency gap between innovation and risk words was relatively narrow, and as one might expect from a financial company, attitudes to risk marginally outweighed attitudes to innovation. The frequency of risk words noticeably dropped between 2007 and 2008 with a corresponding slight dip in the use of innovation-based words. This is interesting since the peak of the Global Financial Crisis is generally considered to have occurred in September 2008 with the bankruptcy of Lehman Brothers and the government bailout of insurance giant AIG.

Since the CCI in 2012, the company has become culturally more risk averse as indicated by the upward and long-term trend in the use of risk words. This subsequent adaptive cultural change has now placed an increased emphasis on risk aversion, personal conduct and citizenship values. Furthermore, the number of innovation related words has remained steady for over 20 years and suggests that Barclays is not creating a culture which encourages innovation even though its current 'values statement' presents "innovation" as fundamental to driving excellence in the organization.[2] The word frequency analysis also provides an interesting insight into how Barclays viewed the COVID-19 global pandemic as a considerable threat to the business with a substantial uplift in the use of risk words in 2020, but also as an unexpected opportunity to rethink its business models, processes, products and innovative solutions for improved efficiency and a more resilient organization.

Whilst Barclays have quite rightly placed cultural change at the center of their transformative process since the CCI in 2012, the increased emphasis on risk aversion may be to the detriment of the types of innovative attitudes and behaviors that drive growth and may go some way to explaining the mixed signals in corporate financial performance. In addition, the company do not disclose R&D expenditure, preventing the calculation of R&D Intensity, a key indicator of innovation.

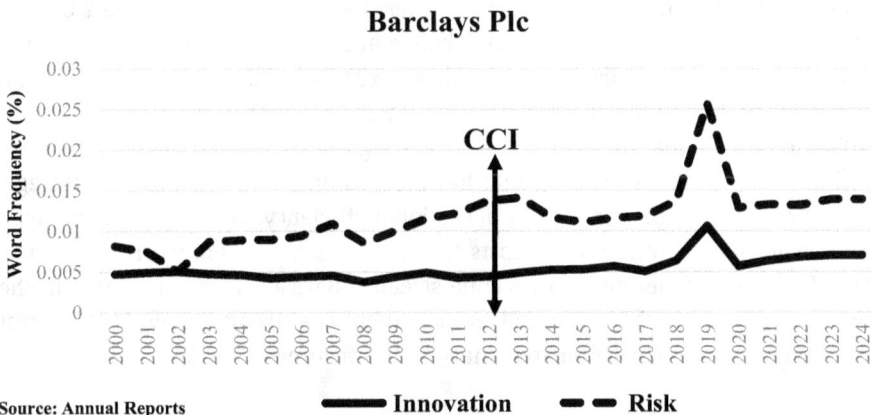

Diagram 4: Cultural Attitudes to Innovation and Risk (2000–2024).

Corporate Financial Performance

The impact of the CCI on Barclays corporate financial performance is, on first exami-nation, not as clear cut as that presented in the previous case study on AIG. While it's recent financial performance appears strong, a deeper analysis reveals a more com-plex picture and one where the underlying macro forces have significantly influenced Barclays in a favorable way, rather than a financial performance solely driven by exe-cuting good business strategy. This is most evident with the impact of Bank of England base interest rates, which had remained at historically low levels during the 2010s, but increased dramatically following a surge in inflation after the COVID-19 pandemic. With global supply chains disrupted and consumer demand rampant, central banks across the globe, including the Bank of England, raised their base interest rates from 0.1% in November 2021 to 5.25% in August 2023. As a consequence, Barclays operating income rose markedly from £3,508 million in 2020, to an incredible £9,030 million in 2021. The increases in interest rates have been a major factor contributing to Barclays "windfall profits"[8] which have resulted in substantial increases in operating income of £8,659 million in 2022, £7,418 million in 2023 and £8,004 million in 2024.

The full year financial returns for Barclays in 2000 were strong. The company had a market capitalization of £36,124 million, revenues of £8,891 million and an operating income of £3,945 million. By 2011, its market capitalization stood at the lower figure of £28,762 million as market sentiment and a loss of public trust turned against financial firms, however, revenue had grown to £25,466 million (a 186% increase since 2000) and operating income to £6,608 million (a 68% increase since 2000). An impressive performance by any measure.

However, the core argument for a case of Corporate Trauma is a comparison of financial performance in the 12 years after the CCI in 2012 (see Table 2 below). From this we see that the percentage 'Change in Post CCI Average since 2012' indi-cates that market capitalization had fallen to £32,930 million (a 19% decline) and that revenue had fallen to £21,057million (a 3% decline). Having said that, the 140% increase in operating income has been significant, driven by an uncompro-mising approach to cost-cutting that has focused on a large number of strategic divestments and improvements in operational efficiency. Whilst the classic turn-around playbook would reduce costs to ensure financial stability, it would also identify ways to generate new revenue streams. Barclays have succeeded in the former and failed in the latter, and as such, there is a strong argument to suggest that the company is struggling to turnaround its fortunes.

Table 2: Barclays Comparative Average Financial Performance (2000–2024).

Source: S&P Capital IQ	Pre-CCI Average (2000–2011)	Critical Corporate Incident (2012)	Post-CCI Average (2013–2024)	Change in Post CCI Average since 2012 (%)
Market Capitalization (GB£ mn)	33,475	40,451	32,930	–19
Revenue (GB£ mn)	16,155	21,697	21,057	–3
Operating Income (GB£ mn)	4,827	2,302	5,515	140

A Transgenerational Response Over Multiple Corporate Generations

CEO Bob Diamond was regarded as a controversial, powerful and wealthy figure in the financial industry, known for an aggressive business style that had characterized him as one of the 'Masters of the Universe'. His short tenure ended with his resignation on 3rd July 2012 in the wake of the interest rate rigging scandal. Further resignations swiftly followed with Chief Operating Officer, Jerry del Missier and Chairman Marcus Agius. Agius, however, returned a day later as (interim) CEO in order to stabilize the bank and restore public confidence following the scandal.[9]

Antony Jenkins was appointed as CEO in August 2012 with a remit to transform and reshape the company by de-risking the business, rebuilding trust, improving operational efficiency and cost control to deliver sustainable financial returns. The overarching theme for this new strategic direction focused on embedding a 'values driven culture' that would deliver on customer needs and build lasting relationships with clients. Jenkins wanted Barclays to be the "Go-To bank of choice for people regardless of the transaction they are looking to make"[10] and believed that driving cultural change by improving governance and enhancing transparency would ensure accountability for performance at all levels of the organization. Jenkins tenure ended in July 2015 having failed to turnaround the company with revenues declining by 12%, and operating income declining by 3% during his three-year term. The board were unhappy with the pace and execution of a transformation strategy that should have improved efficiency and reduced costs. Investors also remained unconvinced with Barclays market capitalization stagnating over the same period. Chairman John McFarlane immediately assumed the role of CEO and commented that "What we need is profit improvement. Barclays is not efficient. We are cumbersome" and that "cultural change was urgently required".[11]

James "Jes" Staley was appointed CEO of Barclays on the 28th October 2015 due to his extensive experience in corporate and investment banking, a crucial area for Barclays strategic repositioning and future direction. Chairman John McFarlane commented that Staley was a "man of enormous integrity, and someone who both understands the business, but also the importance of cultural reform and the need to conduct our business in a way that we can all be proud of".[12] During Staley's tenure revenues declined from £19,641 million in 2015, to £16,945 million by 2020, whilst operating income improved from £2,165 million to £3,508 million over the same period. Staley's tenure focused on improving core business operations and simplifying the structure by creating two divisions, Barclays UK and Barclays Corporate & International, whilst rebuilding its reputation and fostering a strong culture of integrity.

The improvement in operating income was achieved by aggressively running down non-core operations (e.g. Barclays Africa Group Limited) and selling 20 businesses in a number of countries which were no longer strategically important but had caused a "significant drag"[13] on profitability. Staley had been asked by the board to improve operational efficiency, cuts cost and reposition Barclays for a sustainable future. By 2018 much of the company's structural transformation had been achieved. The business was simplified, and operational efficiencies had delivered cost savings of almost £14 billion[14] and operating income had grown from £2,165 million to £5,774 million in just three years. Staley had implemented a classic corporate turnaround strategy by cost-cutting, restructuring the company's operations and selling off non-core assets to improve profitability. However, the scope of Barclays corporate perimeter of activities had contracted and investors remained cautious, with the company's market capitalization falling from £26,568 million in 2015 to £25,582 million in 2020. Staley had been brought in to turn around Barclays and the lingering effects of a corporate crisis that had occurred in 2012. However, his tenure as CEO ended with a corporate crisis where '*he*' was the center of attention. Once considered a "man of enormous integrity" Staley's shock resignation on 1st November 2021 followed a regulatory investigation into the characterization of his relationship with disgraced financier and convicted sex offender Jeffrey Epstein. Staley was found to have misled regulators and was subsequently fined £1.8 million by the Financial Conduct Authority for a serious failure of judgement and failure to act with integrity. He was also deemed to not be "a fit and proper person to perform the role of a CEO or any other senior management function".[15]

Current incumbent, C.S. Venkatakrishnan, was swiftly installed as CEO on 1st November 2021. With significant banking and financial services experience, he had previously served as Barclays Head of Global Markets and Group Chief Risk Officer from 2016 to 2020. Venkatakrishnan's tenure started with managing a severe downturn in consumer business as a result of the ongoing effects of the COVID-19 pandemic. He acknowledged the transformational macro environment forces affecting banking (technology, the growth of the public and private capital markets, and the climate transition) and these drivers of change framed Barclays strategic responses for the next three years. He argued that the "dominant business challenge for the next decade"[16] would be to deliver services digitally in order to compete, not just with other banks, but with a growing number of new non-bank competitors. As such, Venkatakrishnan believed that Barclays needed "an innovative mindset"[16] to deliver on strategic priorities that included: the digital transformation of banking, from consumer services to investment banking; digitalizing customer products, services and experiences to provide convenient and accessible digital services; investing in technology infrastructure to improve efficiency; and supporting the transition to a low-carbon economy.

Venkatakrishnan's tenure to date has been characterized by navigating the company through the effects of macro-uncertainty caused by inflation and geopolitical risks. This uncertainty is reflected in Barclays financial performance between 2021 and 2024, where revenues increased by 7% whilst operating income decreased by 11%. Furthermore, in response to Barclays approach of returning £9 billion to shareholders between 2019 and 2021 and a promise to distribute "at least £10 billion"[17] by 2026, investors have responded favorably which has resulted in an increase in the company's market capitalization of 29% between 2021 and 2024.

In summary, the corporate crisis of 2012 marked a pivotal and detrimental turning point for Barclays, initiating a sustained period of underperformance that has proven resistant to the efforts of successive leadership. This critical event, which significantly impacted the bank's reputation and financial stability, set in motion a series of adaptive and dysfunctional challenges that successive CEOs have not only inherited, but found difficult to manage effectively. Since 2012, Barclays has experienced an unusually high degree of CEO turnover, with five individuals, including two interim appointments, occupying the top executive position. This rapid succession of leaders has resulted in an average tenure of just 2.4 years, a figure that starkly contrasts with the average CEO tenure of 9.3 years across the S&P 500.

Conclusions

The case of Barclays provides an interesting and nuanced picture of the challenges and complexities faced by the company since the rate rigging crisis in 2012. While the bank has made progress in some areas, its ability to raise operating income to pre-crisis levels and regain investor confidence, while maintaining the highest ethical standards, has proven to be a tough ask for successive CEOs. The "values-driven culture" envisioned by Jenkins proved to be a significant challenge. Staley's shock resignation, due to the Epstein affair, presented another major setback for Barclays who had sought to develop a strong ethical culture and accountability at every level of the organization. Staley's tenure was typified by the classic turnaround playbook with a strategic shift towards cutting cost, simplifying the business by divesting non-core assets, and focusing on core areas like investment banking and consumer banking. It almost worked. Staley delivered improvements in operating income through cost-cutting and restructuring, but the growth in operating income and shareholder value creation remained elusive. Current CEO Venkatakrishnan has recognized the critical importance of digital transformation, emphasizing the need to adapt to the changing technological landscape and compete with fintech companies. However, Barclays financial performance during his tenure has, so far, been indifferent.

The evidence presented above provides the underpinning for a number of conclusions that support the notion of Corporate Trauma. Barclays appear to be suffering from a stress reaction to the crisis in 2012 which has created a number of dysfunctional adaptive changes that have had a lasting impact on its reputation, culture and financial performance.

Firstly, Barclays average market capitalization has declined since the CCI on the 27th June 2012. While the company implemented a new values driven strategy in the aftermath of the rate rigging scandal, its long-term share price performance has consistently underperformed when compared to best-in-class industry benchmarks. It is also interesting to note in Venkatakrishnan's statement in 2021 that Barclays' share price over the previous five years had not declined as much as the FTSE 350 UK Bank Index over the same period.[15] For a global banking institution with an aspiration to deliver a "best-in-class customer and client experience"[2] this comparison appeared to be a case of searching for any shred of good PR news following a chronic financial performance. Furthermore, Barclays financial health has experienced a significant deterioration since the CCI. The physiological impact of the trauma is evident in the comparison of financial metrics from before and after the crisis event. The company has seen a decline in average operating income, whilst its market capitalization has seen a substantial decline over a 12-year period, with market sentiment and public trust still clearly unreceptive to the value provided by the company.

Secondly, the CCI of 2012 created an adaptive psychological change on Barclays culture where risk aversion has consistently dominated over innovative thinking. Whilst Venkatakrishnan's vision for a digital transformation of Barclays business operations calls on an innovative mindset to deliver on strategic priorities, these will likely be hindered by the lingering trauma on Barclays culture, particularly given that the explicit reporting on R&D expenditure makes it difficult to assess the true extent of its commitment to developing a culture of innovation.

Thirdly, five CEOs have attempted to turnaround Barclays with strategies that have included: introducing a new purpose and values to drive cultural change; cutting costs and focusing on core business to drive profitability; and a digital transformation to improve operational efficiencies in a dynamic marketplace. Each CEO has inherited the lingering effects of a Corporate Trauma that has manifested in various ways, including a tarnished corporate reputation, a risk-averse organizational culture, and persistent financial underperformance. Consequently, the average tenure of CEOs following a crisis is markedly shorter than the average tenure for CEOs across the S&P 500.

Despite the cost-cutting, restructuring and digital transformation strategies employed by successive CEOs, Barclays has not fully recovered from the crisis of 2012. This suggests that the strategic issues facing the company are deeper than can be addressed by a classic turnaround play. After more than a decade of chronic underperformance and a carousel of CEO's, Barclays has struggled to regain investor trust and the trauma of the LIBOR scandal continues to cast its long shadow.

BlackBerry: Its life Jim, but not as we know it

Background

BlackBerry . . . it's a brand that you may recall with fondness if you had one of their handsets in the late 2000s. But it is not a brand that currently comes top of mind when you think . . . 'smartphone'. The rise and fall of BlackBerry is a clear illustration of the dangers of complacency and a lack of organizational adaptation in fast-moving consumer technology markets. At its peak between 2009 and 2010, BlackBerry was ranked in the top 100 Best Global Brands[1] and had a 20% share of the global smartphone market. It also had a number of high-profile users, most notably, U.S. President Barack Obama. Indeed, on entering the White House he famously said that he didn't want to give in to National Security Agency demands to dispense with using his device, because of fears about hacking, commenting that "I'm still clinging to my BlackBerry . . . and they're going to (have to) pry it out of my hands".[2] Obama, like many other early adopters of the technology brand were showing signs of smartphone addiction, compulsively checking emails and messaging, which led to the popular slang term 'Crackberry'. However, by 2020, its global market share had catastrophically collapsed to 0.02%[3] and now stands at a figure so negligible that it is difficult to express it in a way that's both accurate and meaningful.

BlackBerry, formerly known as 'Research In Motion' was incorporated in 1984 and is headquartered in Waterloo, Canada. As pioneers of wireless data communication and mobile email, their distinctive QWERTY keyboards became enormously popular with business professionals and the emphasis on secure communication and data encryption attracted a considerable number of government users. However, the Apple iPhone revolution marked a step change in smartphone technology with its touchscreen interface and apps allowing consumers to easily access and interact with a wide range of tools and services. BlackBerry struggled to adapt to a rapidly changing market and failed to keep pace with consumer preferences and the innovation levels of its competitors. The company officially announced its decision to stop making its own smartphones in 2016. Today, the company has transitioned into a cybersecurity software and services company. It operates in three market segments (Cybersecurity, Internet of Things, and Licensing) where it leverages AI and machine learning to deliver innovative solutions in the areas of cybersecurity, safety, and data privacy solutions to business and government users worldwide.[4]

A Corporate Crisis: The Trigger that Caused a Downward Spiral

BlackBerry's Critical Corporate Incident (CCI) occurred in early March 2011 with a widely reported conference call made by co-CEO Jim Balsillie who mentioned the imminent arrival of some "powerful new BlackBerrys"[5] early in 2012. Market analysts and investors expressed concern that prematurely hyping these new devices could negatively impact sales of existing BlackBerry models. Balsillie's comment was most likely an attempt to promote the company's product innovation capabilities to investors, analysts and other stakeholders. However, in reality it was an unintentional misstep in strategic communication that had created serious consequences. News spread, and as a result of Balsillie's statement, consumers delayed their purchase of existing BlackBerry products in eager anticipation of the impending launch of a new product range with superior features. BlackBerry had succumbed to the 'Osborne Effect' – phenomenon where customers choose to wait for a new and improved device that leads to a decline in the sales of existing products, which in turn, negatively affects sales revenue. The term originates from the Osborne Computer Corporation who experienced a significant drop in sales of its Osborne 1 computer after announcing that two new models, the Osborne Executive and the Osborne Vixen, would soon be launched into the market.

Customers, anticipating the superior features of the new models, chose to delay their purchase of existing products, ultimately leading to a significant drop in revenue and financial difficulties that led to the company's bankruptcy in the early 1980s.

Within days of the CCI, BlackBerry announced, on the 24th March, that quarterly revenue had fallen short of expectations and warned that a sales drive in the current three-month period would pivot to cheaper models in its product range. The statement to investors also reported that the growth of BlackBerry sales had slowed in North America due to competition from Apple's iPhone and that the recent decline in revenue was not the start of a downward trend. Investors and analysts weren't convinced and market sentiment toward BlackBerry turned with an immediate fall of 11% in its share price.[6]

The initial launch timeline for "the powerful new BlackBerry 10"[5] was overly ambitious and the company's premature announcement damaged its credibility at a time when its existing product range was steadily losing market share. Early 2012 turned into late 2012, with further announcements of production problems leading to more delays in the new product launch. On 30th January 2013, almost two years after Balsillie announced the imminent arrival of a game changing new product, the company launched two new BlackBerry 10 smartphones (all-touch and touch with physical keyboard) which had been "re-designed, re-engineered, and re-invented . . . (to) create a new and unique mobile computing experience".[7] However, technology and market demands had moved on and consumers criticized BlackBerry's new products for their lack of a robust app system compared to iOS and Android products. The BlackBerry 10 struggled to gain traction with consumers and the company's market share in the smartphone market diminished to insignificant levels in the years that followed. Market sentiment also turned against BlackBerry with investors pessimistic about the company's long-term future prospects (see Diagram 5 below).

From a Corporate Trauma perspective, the chronic decline in BlackBerry's share price reflects a severe response 'triggered' by the CCI in early March 2011. The exact date of Balsillie's investor call has not been reported, but the 4th March is the most likely as the company's share price fell by 6.12% that day. The impact of the CCI on BlackBerry's market valuation has been profound and enduring, suggesting a lasting market perception of severe, irreparable damage. This sustained decline indicates that the CCI acted as a decisive blow, inflicting a long-term, debilitating condition that has significantly tarnished BlackBerry's reputation as an innovator. Prior to the CCI, the company had consistently outperformed 'best-in-class' firms throughout 2009 and 2010. This period of success, however, was abruptly reversed following the CCI in March 2011. Since then, BlackBerry's share price has catastrophically collapsed, plummeting by a staggering 92% since

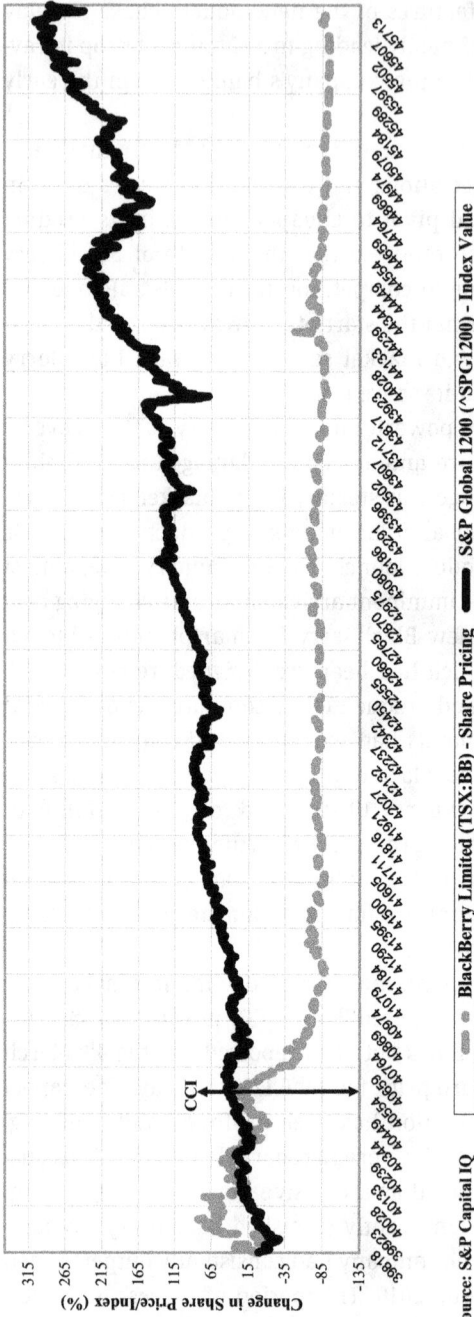

Source: S&P Capital IQ

Legend: •••• BlackBerry Limited (TSX:BB) - Share Pricing —— S&P Global 1200 (^SPG1200) – Index Value

Diagram 5: Share Price Performance of BlackBerry v S&P Global 1200 Index (2009–2025).

the date of the CCI. This dramatic decline stands in stark contrast to the broader market's performance, as represented by the S&P Global 1200 Index, which witnessed a substantial 169% increase in value during the same timeframe.[8]

An Adverse Modification in Corporate Culture

Corporate Trauma examines the psychological marker of cultural attitudes to 'innovation' and 'risk' which are fundamental to an organizations health, development and long-term growth. A crisis can, however, significantly derail innovation-led growth strategies as organizations grapple with survival and protecting their corporate reputation. The analysis of BlackBerry's attitudes to innovation and risk (see Diagram 6 below) over the period 2000 and 2024 provides a fascinating insight into the cultural dynamics of a company that rapidly rose to global dominance in the smartphone market and fell to insignificance just as quickly.

Between 2000 and 2006, the frequency gap between innovation and risk words was clearly pronounced as one would expect from a company competing in an emerging smartphone industry. In the early stages of growth, this industry was characterized by uncertainty and a high potential for innovation. The lack of established products and technologies created a dynamic environment ready for groundbreaking companies to achieve first-mover advantage and market differentiation. The Global Financial Crisis no doubt undermined levels of creative thinking and a commitment to innovation between 2007 and 2010. However, in 2011 the gap between the frequency use of innovation and risk words suggests that BlackBerry was culturally more attuned to prioritizing innovation as a strategic driver to achieve competitiveness and long-term growth. Conversely, the word frequency analysis indicates that the CCI in 2011 appears to have triggered an adaptive and sustained psychological change in BlackBerry's culture with the company becoming more risk averse, as indicated by the upward and long-term trend in the use of risk words compared to the declining use of innovation-based words. Indeed, since the CCI in 2011, the number of risk words had increased by 96%, and innovation words by just 5% over the period to 2020.[3] Currently, the gap between innovation and risk word frequencies has closed to the point where any proposed innovative activity is viewed by BlackBerry in almost the same terms as risk. Furthermore, a widely held view in business and management literature indicates that higher levels of R&D expenditure improves growth prospects and corporate financial performance. In the 11 years prior to the CCI, BlackBerry's R&D Intensity averaged at 9.14%, which is comparable to the 12.6% for the most innovative companies in the world (Alphabet, Amazon, Apple, Microsoft and Tesla) who are known to be culturally orientated toward innovation. In comparison to the 13 years post the CCI, BlackBerry's R&D Intensity has averaged at an incredible 21.96% almost as high as Tesla's equivalent commitment to R&D at 25.90% of sales revenue over the period 2000 and 2023.[9] As we shall see in the following section, this commitment to R&D has not translated into healthy financial returns and may be indicative of BlackBerry's efforts not being aligned with actual market needs or consumer demands, poor execution in product development, or effective sales and marketing implementation.

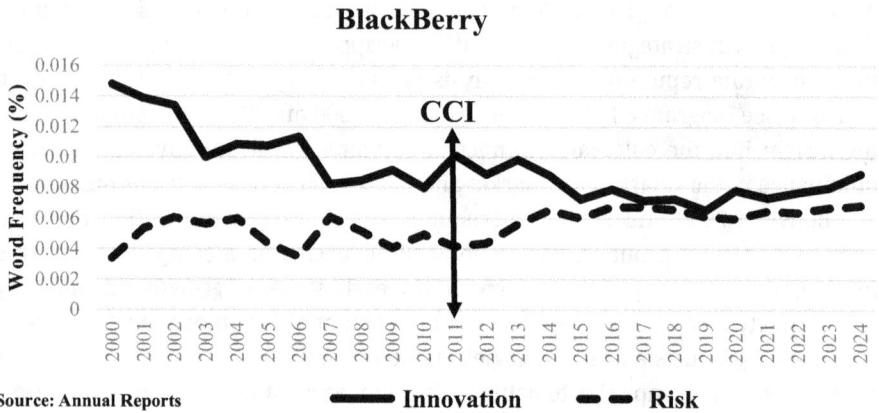

Diagram 6: Cultural Attitudes to Innovation and Risk (2000–2024).

Corporate Financial Performance

For a company that was once a global leader in the smartphone industry, their financial performance following the CCI in 2011 makes for difficult reading. Over the period 2011 to 2024, BlackBerry's market capitalization plummeted from US$29,730 million to US$1,712 million. A staggering decline in market value and a severe loss of investor confidence and shareholder wealth. Furthermore, revenues collapsed from US$19,907 million to US$853 million, and operating income from US$4,636 million to a loss of US$35 million between 2011 to 2024. This catastrophic failure to generate significant levels of revenue and profit is a clear sign that the company has failed to adapt to emerging technologies, changing consumer preferences and a dynamic competitive landscape. Since 2011, BlackBerry have had a rather insular view of the world, with successive annual statements articulating how Blackberry 'had' revolutionized the mobile communications industry. Incredibly, in 2016, they reported that its "products and services are widely recognized in the market for productivity and security" and that it believed it delivered "the most secure end to-end mobile enterprise solutions in the market".[3] In the same year, the company reported that operating income had fallen by 73% over the course of the financial year; yet another indication that its products had little in the way of relevance in the marketplace.

BlackBerry's financial performance describes a company facing severe challenges and raises fundamental questions about its mission, values, and strategic direction. The competitive threats, changing market dynamics and declining customer demand are not just temporary issues, but deep-seated strategic challenges that threaten the core of BlackBerry's purpose and its ability to survive and thrive. The Corporate Trauma created by the CCI on the 4th March 2011 triggered a downward spiral in corporate financial performance (see Table 3 below) with the key physiological markers from 'before and after' the crisis indicating the scale of the damage. The average market capitalization over the course of 11 years prior to the CCI was US$19,637 million, compared to US$4,492 million in the 13 years after the crisis. Equally, average revenue had only grown by 4%, from US$3,635 million to US$3,778 million over the same period. Most disconcertingly, is the comparison of average operating income which had decreased from US$883 million to a loss of US$274 million.

The starkest evidence of Corporate Trauma is the company's financial performance as indicated by the percentage 'Change in Post CCI Average since 2011'. The financial fallout following the crisis has been nothing short of devastating. An 85% decline in market capitalization signifies a massive loss of investor value and confidence. The 81% drop in revenue points to a severe disruption of core business operations and a drastically reduced ability to generate income. The extraordinary 106% decline in operating income underscores that the company is not only less profitable but is actively losing substantial amounts of money from its

Table 3: BlackBerry Comparative Average Financial Performance (2000–2024).

Source: S&P Capital IQ	Pre-CCI Average (2000–2010)	Critical Corporate Incident (2011)	Post-CCI Average (2012–2024)	Change in Post CCI Average since 2011 (%)
Market Capitalization (US$ mn)	19,637	29,730	4,492	−85
Revenue (US$ mn)	3,635	19,907	3,778	−81
Operating Income (US$ mn)	883	4,636	(274)	−106

operations. The crisis has triggered a financial implosion, signaling profound and potentially existential challenges for BlackBerry. As Mr. Spock, the fictional character from Star Trek might have dryly commented . . . 'its life Jim, but not as we know it'.

A Transgenerational Response Over Multiple Corporate Generations

Co-CEOs, and founders, Mike Lazaridis and Jim Balsillie are credited with building a successful and influential technology company that revolutionized mobile communication in the 2000s. Their leadership during the early part of their 20-year tenure at BlackBerry laid the foundation for its initial success and established it as a major player in the global smartphone industry. Lazaridis was responsible for the development of the company's core technology and product innovation, whilst Balsillie concentrated on business strategy, operations, sales and marketing. This division of responsibilities allowed each executive to leverage their respective strengths and drive BlackBerry's global expansion. Having said that, some analysts at the time suggested that this co-CEO structure may have contributed to a lack of decisive decision-making which may have hindered the company's ability to adapt to rapidly changing market dynamics and the emergence of formidable players like Apple and Google. Lazaridis and Balsillie resigned on 22nd January 2012 saying that it was "the right time to pass the baton to new leadership"[10] after significant declines in sales, market share and market capitalization.

Thorsten Heins was immediately appointed CEO. He had been the Chief Operating Officer for product and sales and was regarded as an executive with the necessary leadership skills and industry experience to drive the company forward in what was a rapidly changing marketplace. His strategy focused on ensuring the successful launch of the BlackBerry 10 platform, whilst leveraging the brand to drive global subscriber growth.[11] However, his tenure was short lived and he stepped down on the 4th November 2013 after failing to reverse the company's rapid decline from a market-leading position. A 50% market share in the U.S. in 2009 had fallen to less than a 3% share just four years later. The once celebrated brand was on the brink of collapse. It had failed to adapt to the evolving needs of consumers and businesses and competition from players using the two dominant mobile operating systems, Android and iOS. As a consequence, the company's financial performance rapidly deteriorated with operating income plummeting from US$1,977 million in 2012, to a loss of US$680 million a year later. Significant cost-cutting measures followed, including laying-off a quarter of its workforce.[12]

John Chen was appointed CEO on the 4th November 2013 with a clear remit to revive the company's fortunes. As the former CEO of Sybase, a computer database software company, he had turned it around from being a company that had lost US$98 million in 1998, to one that was sold for US$5.8 billion just two years later. Chen confidently predicted that it would take 18 months to turn around Black-Berry and that he had "done this before and seen the same movie before".[13]

Chen immediately set about repositioning BlackBerry by changing its focus to enterprise customers, particularly in regulated industries where security features were a key consideration. He also changed the organizational structure, with four strategic business units operating in differentiated markets that were positioned around the key product offerings of security, productivity and communications.[14] Between 2014 and 2016, BlackBerry pivoted its strategy, focusing heavily on the enterprise market. Leveraging its strong foundation in security by developing and offering a suite of enterprise software and services designed to meet the evolving needs of businesses in a rapidly changing mobile communications landscape. The company also capitalized on the emerging Internet of Things sectors by innovating software solutions for connected vehicles and other embedded systems. Chen cut costs and improved operating income, from a loss of US$3,526 million in 2014, to a loss of US$458 million in 2016. However, the move to reposition the company to compete in niche markets had no doubt contributed to a significant fall in revenues, from US$6,813 million to US$2,160 million over the same period. While reduced losses are a positive turnaround sign, a substantial revenue drop raised concerns about BlackBerry's overall financial health and long-term sustainability. A successful turnaround typically involves not just improving profitability but also demonstrating sustainable revenue growth and overall financial strength. It also involves fostering a culture of innovation and adaptability and whilst Chen had increased BlackBerry's commitment to innovation, by increasing R&D Intensity annually to 17.8%, 19.2% and 21.7% between 2014 and 2016, this didn't appear to have had a positive influence on sales revenue. Furthermore, the gap between innovation and risk word frequencies continued to close (see Diagram 6 above). Chen's initial prediction of an 18-month turnaround was proven to be too optimistic and finding the way out of the maze of corporate decline had proved to be more challenging than originally thought. He may have seen the movie before, but this time, the ending was different!

Between 2017 and 2023 Chen had strategically positioned the company to capitalize on developing solutions for securing and managing the increasing number of connected devices by expanding into new Internet of Things markets; and diversified revenue streams through a focus on enterprise software, cybersecurity services, and technology licensing. The acquisition of Cylance in 2019 also brought advanced AI and machine learning capabilities to BlackBerry's security portfolio, with Chen commenting that in making the purchase "BlackBerry took a giant step forward toward our goal of being the world's largest and most trusted AI-cybersecurity company".[15]

Without much warning, Chen announced to staff on the 30th October 2023 that he was retiring after 10 years at the helm. He noted that he had achieved all three of the priorities he set when first taking up his tenure as CEO. These were to: stabilize the finances to avoid bankruptcy; develop and execute a new strategic direction; establish a foundation for the company's long-term growth.[16] However, BlackBerry's corporate financial performance during Chen's tenure, between 2013 and 2023, tells a different story: market capitalization had fallen 65%, from US$7,645 million to US$2,668 million; revenue had fallen 94% from US$11,073 million to US$656 million; whilst operating income showed an improvement by reducing the size of losses, from US$680 million to US$217 million. Furthermore, during Chen's tenure BlackBerry reported losses in every year, with the exception of 2015. From a Corporate Trauma perspective, a number matters question the veracity of Chen's claim of a successful turnaround. The decline in market capitalization is a clear signal that investors had lost confidence in BlackBerry, and the decline in revenue raises a serious question over the company's ability to generate sales. Chen also claimed that the company "is unquestionably innovative"[16] and he backed up his commitment to innovation with an average R&D Intensity figure of 23.2% during his tenure. Essentially, BlackBerry had 'thrown the kitchen sink' at product and service innovation in AI, Machine Learning, cybersecurity and embedded systems in order to gain a competitive edge. This significant commitment to R&D is indicative of typical moonshot projects which require significant time and resource investment before yielding a return on sales revenues, operating income and investor confidence.

Chen's surprise announcement meant that long-term board director Richard Lynch was appointed as interim Chief Executive Officer on the 4th November 2023. He had previously served as Chief Technology Officer of Verizon Communications and Verizon Wireless. However, his tenure lasted just a matter of weeks.

John J. Giamatteo was subsequently appointed CEO on the 11th December 2023 having served as the President of BlackBerry's Cybersecurity business since October 2021. With a wealth of industry experience with technology companies, including McAfee and AVG Technologies, Giamatteo was regarded as the ideal candidate to drive the re-structuring of the business that would see BlackBerry separate its Internet of Things and Cybersecurity strategic business units, streamline its centralized functions and aim to grow profits.[17] By the financial year end 2024, Giamatteo had grown revenue from US$656 million to US$853 million, and reduced losses from US$217 million to US$35 million.

In summary, the year 2011 marked an important turning point for Black-Berry, triggered by a crisis that led to a sustained decline in performance. Over the past 13 years, BlackBerry have had five CEOs, including the co-CEO partnership of Lazaridis and Balsillie and one interim appointment. This turnover has resulted in an average CEO tenure of just 2.6 years, which is well below the average of 9.3 years for CEOs within the S&P 500. The persistent failure to reverse the company's decline indicates that the issues stemming from the 2011 crisis are deeply rooted and appear to have been inherited by successive CEOs who have experienced significant problems in revitalizing a company that has struggled to adapt and innovate effectively in a rapidly changing market.

Conclusions

BlackBerry's downfall exemplifies the danger of complacency in rapidly evolving technology markets. Their initial success and market dominance could not be sustained. A failure to adapt to changing consumer preferences and technological advancements, particularly the shift to touchscreen interfaces and apps. The timing of the CCI was particularly damaging because it coincided with a mounting competitive threat from Android and iOS players who surreptitiously took advantage of BlackBerry's self-inflicted Osborne Effect.

The CCI in March 2011 appears to have been a pivotal moment for BlackBerry, triggering a stress reaction that has created a long-term decline in organizational performance and reputation. All of which has been inherited by successive CEOs. The evidence presented above identifies a number of adaptive physiological and psychological markers that support the argument of Corporate Trauma and enables the following conclusions to be made.

Firstly, the physiological financial markers demonstrate how BlackBerry's share price performance has collapsed since the date of the CCI. When compared against the S&P Global 1200 Index, the company's plummeting market capitalization is a clear sign of ill health, a destruction of shareholder wealth and a severe loss of investor confidence. Furthermore, the company's inability to generate healthy levels of revenue demonstrates a fundamental failure to adapt to a rapidly changing market and points to a disconnect between BlackBerry's product offerings and evolving consumer needs and technological advancements. The comparison of corporate financial performance metrics, before and after the CCI, provides evidence of an impact that has resulted in sustained losses.

Secondly, the psychological marker of cultural attitudes to innovation and risk indicates an adaptive response triggered by the crisis. Before the CCI, Black-Berry prioritized innovation, as evidenced by the higher frequency of 'innovation' related words in its annual reports. After the CCI, a clear shift towards risk aversion is observed, with an increase in the use of 'risk' related words over a sustained period. Remarkably, John Chen's resignation letter stated that BlackBerry were "unquestionably innovative"[16], and yet, a company once famed for its innovation-led growth strategy had become more defensive and risk-averse. Despite the cultural shift towards risk aversion, BlackBerry's R&D Intensity actually increased significantly after the CCI. The increased R&D spending, coupled with poor financial performance, implies that the company's innovation efforts are not being translated into successful products that meet consumer needs. The paradox for BlackBerry is that they are spending more on R&D, and yet, are achieving less in terms of market success.

Thirdly, the evidence of adaptive psychological and physiological responses after the CCI provides strong support for a Corporate Trauma that has been inherited by successive CEOs. Despite Chen's claim of a successful turnaround, the continued decline in market capitalization and revenue suggests that the trauma from the initial crisis event continues to impact the company. There is no doubt that his strategy repositioned BlackBerry on enterprise customers and niche markets, but these did no not lead to sustainable revenue growth. In many ways, Chen's 10-year tenure is a surprise given that the company returned a profit in just one of those years. The Board of Directors may have believed in Chen's long-term vision and strategy, and while not yielding sustained revenue results, progress had been made in repositioning the company and making it a leaner operation in terms of costs. They may have thought that changing leadership mid-stream would disrupt the strategy and set the company back even further. However, his sudden resignation, with no immediate successor in place, may have been an indication that the turnaround had not been fully delivered.

The 'its life Jim, but not as we know it' analogy mentioned earlier, captures the essence of BlackBerry's Corporate Trauma. While the company still exists, it is a shadow of its former self, operating in a vastly different competitive landscape to the one it dominated in 2009 and where the consequences of complacency and the crisis in 2011 have left a toxic legacy of trauma.

BP: Deepwater Horizon's Lingering Shadow

Background

Transitioning from a legacy oil producer into to an integrated energy company presents a complex set of strategic challenges that make both planning a clear transition strategy and executing it a significant undertaking. British Petroleum

PLC (BP) is no exception and balancing its existing oil and gas operations with investments in renewable energy sources has been anything but a smooth transition. Indeed, the company signaled its aim to move to renewable energy as far back as 2000 with the then CEO, John Browne, launching the "Beyond Petroleum"[1] campaign. More recently, over the past five years BP have driven an ambitious strategy to diversify away from fossil fuels and so in many ways the company's announcement in February 2025 that it was rowing back on its green energy transition came as a surprise. BP's CEO stated that the company's "optimism for a fast transition was misplaced and we went too far, too fast"[2] and that it was time to "reset BP, with an unwavering focus on growing long-term shareholder value"[3] by increasing upstream investment and production. Given that BP has a long history marked by significant strategic transformations, it's inability to navigate the complexities of the 21st century energy landscape was seen as a backward step that essentially kept shareholders contented in the short-term.

BP can trace its roots back to the Anglo-Persian Oil Company which was founded in 1908 in order to exploit oil discoveries in Persia (now Iran). William Knox D'Arcy, a British businessman, secured the initial oil concession and the British government became a major shareholder in 1914 after recognizing the strategic importance of a vast oil supply for the Royal Navy, which at the time was a formidable global force. BP's first major transformation emerged in 1954 when the board changed the name to the British Petroleum Company, and throughout the 20th century, BP grew into a major international energy company through numerous mergers and acquisitions, most significantly with the U.S. firm Amoco in 1998. The deal transformed BP into one of the world's largest oil companies.

In 2024, BP generated revenues of US\$185,408 million from its Gas & Low Carbon Energy, Oil Production & Operations, and Customers & Products segments. Whilst the company's low carbon business includes solar, offshore and onshore wind, hydrogen, carbon capture and storage, and power trading of renewable energy. As such, the recent strategic "reset" represents a significant setback for this business unit and the company's wider green energy transformation ambitions.

A Corporate Crisis: The Trigger that Caused a Downward Spiral

At approximately 9.49pm[4] on the 20th April 2010 a significant moment in BP's history occurred. An explosion on the Deepwater Horizon drilling platform killed 11 workers, seriously injured others and started the largest marine oil spill in U.S. history[5], releasing millions of barrels of crude oil into the Gulf of Mexico. The fire raged for two days before the rig sank. Airplanes sprayed millions of gallons of surface and subsea dispersants. Hundreds of controlled fires were used to dispel surface oil. Fisheries were closed in federal waters. BP started drilling a relief well alongside the failed Macondo oil well and pumped thousands of barrels of mud to plug the leak. It failed. Tens of thousands of responders were deployed to the Gulf Coast for a containment and clean-up operation. The media images of the Deepwater Horizon disaster were powerful and quickly captured global attention. An oil rig engulfed in flames with thick plumes of black smoke rising into the sky. Aerial photographs of the oil slick spreading across the Gulf of Mexico. Oil-soaked birds and marine animals struggling to survive. It was a scene of utter devastation. A picture of hell.

Enter, BP CEO Tony Hayward. The public face of the company and the man responsible for guiding the company through the crisis and restoring public trust. Whilst he apologized for the disruption the explosion had caused, he uttered five words that will no doubt haunt him for the rest of his life . . . "I'd like my life back"[6]. His statement created an image of a detached and uncaring executive, more concerned about his own personal discomfort than the immense suffering of those directly affected by the castastrophe. It was a PR disaster every bit as big as the explosion itself.

The 20th April 2010 is the date of BP's Critical Corporate Incident (CCI). The Deepwater Horizon explosion created short-term effects and long-term consequences that resulted in a trauma which continues to hamper the company's ability to fully recover. The immediate effects of the crisis saw BP's shares fall by 48%[7] in the weeks following the disaster. It was a catastrophic collapse in shareholder value which mirrored the scale of the containment and clean-up efforts which had continued until the oil well was sealed on 19th September 2010.[4] On the 22nd May 2010, U.S. President Barack Obama announced the creation of the 'National Commission on the BP Deepwater Horizon Oil Spill and Offshore Drilling' to identify the causes of the disaster. He followed this up with an address to the nation from the Oval Office on the 15th June saying "make no mistake . . . we will make BP pay for the damage their company has caused".[8]

The National Commission's report[4] found that the "revenue generation enjoyed both by industry and government became the dominant objective" and that "revenue increases depended on moving drilling further offshore and into much deeper waters came with a corresponding increase in the safety and environmental risks of such drilling". They concluded that the "mistakes and oversights at Macondo [oil well] can be traced back to a single overarching failure – a failure of management".

The longer-term consequences of the CCI included a number of substantial and complex financial penalties imposed on BP for the Deepwater Horizon crisis. This included a US$20.8 billion fine on the 4th April 2016 for breaching the Clean

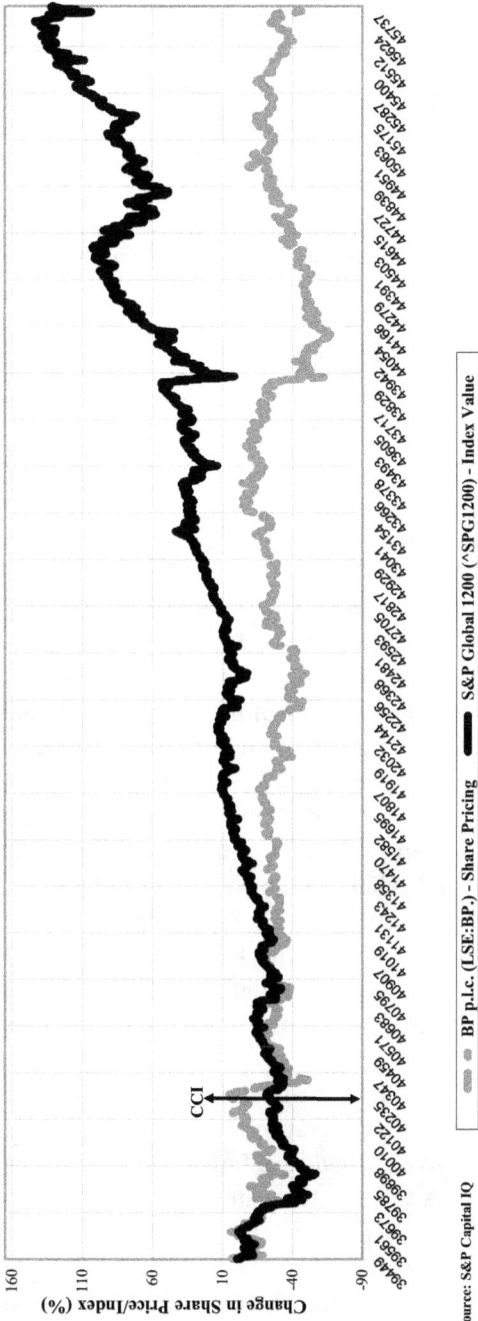

Source: S&P Capital IQ

Diagram 7: Share Price Performance of BP v S&P Global 1200 Index (2008–2025).

Water Act, RESTORE Act, and Oil Pollution Act. It was the largest environment damage settlement in U.S. history.[9] Moreover, the total cost of the crisis has been estimated at US$65 billion including the cost of the initial response, containment efforts, grants to the Gulf states, claims paid and legal costs.[10,11] The substantial costs of the crisis has had a lasting impact on the company's share price and has resulted in a drag on BP's financial performance and investor confidence. It also created uncertainty about the company's future profitability and ability to generate returns for shareholders (see Diagram 7). As the company entered 2010, it had consistently outperformed the S&P Global 1200 Index for more than two years. However, the crisis started a long-term decline of 47% in BP's share price since the date of the CCI, whilst the value of the 'best-in-class' companies has increased by 195%.[12] It is a convincing physiological marker of a Corporate Trauma that reflects a severe response 'triggered' by the CCI on the 20th April 2010.

An Adverse Modification in Corporate Culture

Unlike other case studies presented in this chapter, where there have been examples of risk aversion superseding innovation efforts (i.e. AIG, Barclays and Wells Fargo) and the opposite, where innovative thinking exceeds risk aversion (i.e. BlackBerry, and VW), the word frequency analysis of BP's corporate annual reports demonstrate that, for the most part, innovation and risk are closely aligned and move in tandem. The National Commission's report on the Deepwater Horizon explosion found that whilst BP's safety documentation aimed to promote "no accidents, no harm to people and no damage to the environment" the company did not have "consistent and reliable risk-management processes" and that "BP's safety lapses have been chronic".[4] It is a damming indictment that reveals a significant disconnect between BP's publicly stated commitment to safety and their actual operational practices and highlights wide-ranging failures in risk management and a culture that did not adequately prioritize safety.

Fast forward three years and in their letters to shareholders, the Chairman and CEO announced that 2014 had been a crucial year for BP. The 2014 spike in the use of innovation and risk words is striking and re-enforces the fact that the company had been actively addressing its safety culture and effective risk management processes in the aftermath of the Deepwater Horizon accident (see Diagram 8 below). Indeed, BP's senior executives stated that the company had "taken a major step in refocusing the company after the tragic events of 2010" and that it had now "completed the 10-point plan we had set out in 2011 to make BP a safer, stronger, better performing business" and that the company had "reduced safety-related incidents".[13] Furthermore, it's interesting to note that during a time of focused attention on safety and risk management processes that the use of risk words did not significantly exceed the use of innovation words. This suggests that BP views the exploration and production of offshore oil as inherently innovative and risky, or, that they are actively managing risk in their innovation efforts. It is also worth pointing out that, after the 2014 spike, the use of both words returns to a more stable pattern, similar to the pre-2009 period which raises an important question. Has there really been an adverse and sustained modification in the communication of cultural attitudes to innovation and risk as a result of the crisis?

Where we have seen an adverse modification in cultural attitudes to innovation since the crisis is in BP's investment in R&D. Over the period 2000 to 2009, the company's annual R&D Intensity averaged at 0.20%, and in 2010 it reached 0.26%. However, between 2011 and 2024 the company's R&D Intensity had fallen to an average of 0.18%. This decline indicates an adaptive and persistent change in the company's resource allocation towards R&D, triggered by the crisis in 2010. There's no doubt that the long-term consequences of the multi-billion-dollar regulatory penalties, and the wider costs attributed to the clean-up, operational recovery and legal expenses have resulted in financial constraints that have limited BP's ability to fund R&D activities. It is a clear indicator of Corporate Trauma.

BP

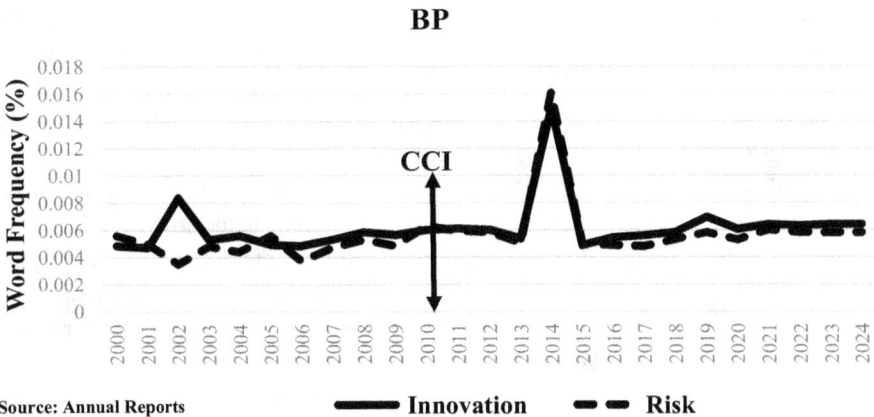

Source: Annual Reports ⸺ **Innovation** ▬ ▬ **Risk**

Diagram 8: Cultural Attitudes to Innovation and Risk (2000–2024).

Corporate Financial Performance

The analysis of BP's share price performance against the S&P Global 1200 Index demonstrates a long-term and strategic drift against best-in-class companies since the date of the CCI. This comparative analysis also provides a broader context to assess BP's financial performance.

The key physiological markers of the Corporate Trauma from 'before and after' the CCI in 2010 indicate a substantial downturn in corporate financial performance. With an average market capitalization of US$76,660 million in the 14 years following the crisis, this figure is 31% lower than the average market capitalization of US$111,800 million over the period 2000 to 2009. Furthermore, the comparison of operating income over the same period shows a decline of 38% from US$21,804 million to US$13,543 million. The revenue performance from 'before and after' the CCI is the only positive outcome, with a 10% improvement in performance. However, this improvement can be explained by the fluctuating global energy market, particularly the prices of oil and gas, where the primary driver for the substantial increase in revenues (up by 53%) and operating income (up by 223%) between 2021 and 2022 was attributed to the rebound in demand from after the initial impact of the COVID-19 pandemic and the subsequent Russia-Ukraine war which caused a sharp increase in oil and gas prices. The UK government introduced the Energy (Oil and Gas) Profits Levy[14] in 2022 which resulted in a 25% levy on ring fence profits of oil and gas companies in response to unusually high prices that meant oil and gas companies were benefiting from windfall profits.

Moreover, the most striking marker of Corporate Trauma on the company's financial performance is the comparison of the financial metrics which analyze the percentage 'Change in Post CCI Average since 2010'. This comparison shows that market capitalization has fallen by 16%, revenue has declined by 16% and operating income has fallen by an astonishing 50%. It's a considerable deterioration in financial performance. It isn't a minor setback. It suggests fundamental issues are at play, particularly, in terms of the company's strategic direction and operational efficiency. Additionally, this deterioration in performance has eroded investor confidence, and a long-term decline in market capitalization which led to the announcement that BP Chair, Helge Lund, would be stepping down after pressure from activist investors who were unhappy about the company's lackluster financial performance.[15]

Table 4: BP Comparative Average Financial Performance (2000–2024).

Source: S&P Capital IQ	Pre-CCI Average (2000–2009)	Critical Corporate Incident (2010)	Post-CCI Average (2011–2024)	Change in Post CCI Average since 2010 (%)
Market Capitalization (US$ mn)	111,800	91,007	76,660	−16
Revenue (US$ mn)	225,259	297,107	248,450	−16
Operating Income (US$ mn)	21,804	26,914	13,543	−50

A Transgenerational Response Over Multiple Corporate Generations

After three years as the CEO of BP, Tony Hayward stepped down on the 1st October 2010 saying that "BP will be a changed company as a result of Macondo [oil well] and it is right that it should embark on its next phase under new leadership".[16] His handling of the crisis was widely perceived as a public relations failure and drew heavy criticism from the public, media, and politicians who claimed that he was insensitive, condescending, out-of-touch, and downplayed the severity of the disaster. It was a failure in leadership on his part and a failure in public relations, exacerbated by a communication strategy which was slow, reactive, and ineffective in conveying empathy and a sense of urgency.

Bob Dudley was appointed CEO on the 1st October 2010. He was a BP board director and responsible for the clean-up operations and compensation programs in the Gulf of Mexico. With a wealth of executive experience in the oil industry he was regarded as "a robust operator in the toughest circumstances".[16] Dudley apologized for the unprecedented scale of the disaster and re-enforced the company's commitment to fulfilling its obligations and that he would "do everything necessary to ensure BP is a company that can be trusted by shareholders and communities around the world".[17] He also announced the sale of up to US$30 billion in assets, $22 billion of disposals, a cut back on discretionary capital spending, cancelled dividends in 2010 and additional credit lines. Dudley's immediate actions had shifted the focus of the company away from growth and shareholder returns, to a financial restructuring that aimed to ensure the long-term viability of BP. The company were in a critical situation and implementing a comprehensive strategy focused on immediate cash generation, cost reduction, and securing financial flexibility would help it survive the crisis.

Dudley did indeed prove to be a robust operator. During his early years in charge he continued to acknowledge the human cost of the Deepwater Horizon disaster, expressing sorrow for the lives lost and the impact on families and communities. He also re-enforced the company's efforts to restore BP's reputation and its attempts to regain trust through transparency, cooperation with investigators, a commitment to responsible operations and improving risk management practices. In 2011, Dudley set out a new strategic direction for the company with a three-year "10-point plan focused on building value for shareholders" which would result in BP becoming a "simpler and more focused as a result of a major divestment programme".[18] He added that the plan would also generate billions of dollars to re-invest in the company's strengths. By 2014, Dudley stated that the plan had been successfully implemented and that "compared with three years ago, we have reduced safety-related incidents, delivered strong operating efficiencies and met our target to increase operating cash flow by more than 50%".[19] Dudley lived up to his reputation as a strong and dependable CEO. He guided BP through a catastrophic event, made efforts to learn from mistakes, made a commitment to affected stakeholders and secured the company's long-term future. The financial impact of the crisis during his tenure, however, reflects a company in severe financial distress: revenue had fallen by 58%, from US$376,157 million to US$158,109 million; and operating income had fallen by 43%, from US$27,428 million to US$15,660 million. After 9-years as CEO, Dudley announced that he would step down and retire in early 2020 after 40-years working at BP.

Bernard Looney, who had led BP's Upstream business, was appointed CEO on the 5th February 2020. BP's Chair commented that Looney was "creative and not bound by traditional ways of working"[20] and the ideal candidate to lead and transform the company through the changing global energy landscape. Looney's tenure was marked by an ambitious and ongoing transformation of BP into an integrated energy company in response to the need for a lower-carbon future and achieving net zero emissions by 2050. "Performing while Transforming" became the mantra which highlighted a dual focus on maintaining current operational performance and profitability, while simultaneously undergoing the "most wide-ranging reorganization for more than a century"[21] to become a more diversified and integrated energy company. BPs' strategic transformation efforts received an unexpected boost from two macro-events that underscored the need for a balanced energy system that was lower carbon, secure, and affordable. The COVID-19 Pandemic had a profound impact on the global demand for oil and gas which combined with the impact of the Russia-Ukraine War had created a high level of uncertainty and volatility in energy markets. These events boosted market sentiment positively, with BP's market capitalization increasing by 57% following a revenue increase of 126% and operating income by 491% between 2020 and 2022. BP's strategic transformation was on course . . . what could possibly go wrong? Looney resigned with immediate effect on the 12th September 2023 following an investigation into his relationships with colleagues at BP. He commented that he had not been "not fully transparent in his previous disclosures" and that he accepts that he was "obligated to make a more complete disclosure".[22] The BP Chair's observation about Looney's unconventional work style took on a significant irony in hindsight.

Murray Auchincloss, BP's Chief Financial Officer was immediately installed as the company's interim CEO and subsequently appointed to the role permanently on the 17th January 2024. BP's Chair commented that Auchincloss's "assured leadership . . . will serve well as we continue our disciplined transformation to an integrated energy company".[23] While the first 12 months of Auchincloss's tenure focused on continuing BP's transition, major shareholders became increasingly disillusioned by the returns from the company's significant investments in renewable energy sources, as well as the consistent underperformance of its share price compared to rivals such as Shell, Chevron and Exxon Mobil. In February 2025, Auchincloss announced that BP would pivot back to its traditional oil and gas exploration business arguing that the pace of the transition had been too fast and that the board had opted for a "reset" and that its focus on green energy had been "misplaced".[3] The company had prioritized short-term shareholder value through increased upstream investment and production and abandoned its transformation into an integrated renewables company. In the wake of the strategic U-turn and shareholder revolt, BP Chair Helge Lund announced that he intended to step down. Having been closely associated with the renewables energy transition strategy and the appointment of two CEOs (Looney and Auchincloss) his judgement had been called into question and continuing in his role was no longer realistic.

Auchincloss went on to argue that the company were now aiming to more than double its market capitalization to a valuation that "echoes the company's valuation prior to the 2010 Deepwater Horizon disaster".[24] Investor's, however, remained unconvinced with Auchincloss's performance, having overseen a 10% decline in revenue and a 61% fall in operating income between 2023 and 2024. As a result, BP's market capitalization had fallen by 17% over the same period. Further pressure was placed on Auchincloss with the profits halving in the first quarter of 2025, the third time in five quarters that the company had missed its profit forecast. The company subsequently announced that its Head of Strategy and a key player in BP's transition to net zero would be stepping down, and in a surprise move, would not be replaced with the role being integrated into other functions.[25]

The impact of the CCI on 20th April 2010 has had a profound and lasting impact on the company's leadership, financial performance, and strategic priorities. BP has struggled to consistently define and execute a long-term strategic direction in the face of significant internal and external pressures. Although Dudley's tenure comes close to that of CEO's in the S&P500, the subsequent level of leadership instability has been a recurring issue, with each CEO having to deliver on a different strategic focus. The average tenure of BP's three CEOs since the crisis in 2010 is just 4.66 years, which is short when compared to the S&P 500 average of 9.3 years. Consecutive CEOs have been unable to turnaround BP as the Corporate Trauma caused by the crisis in 2010 has left a legacy of substantial financial penalties that have caused a drag on the company financial performance, compounded by a failed strategic transformation and a lack of investor confidence.

Conclusions

The Deepwater Horizon disaster of 2010 was a pivotal and traumatic event for BP. It triggered a long-term negative impact across multiple facets of the company that include ongoing challenges in leadership stability, strategic direction, and investor confidence. The evidence detailed above forms the basis for a set of conclusions that support the notion of Corporate Trauma.

Firstly, the physiological financial markers demonstrate that BP's long-term share price performance, when compared to best-in-class benchmarks, has consistently underperformed since the CCI 15-years ago. It is a clear marker of trauma and one that is underpinned by BP's financial performance which shows a remarkable decline in market capitalization, revenue, and operating income. Essentially, BP is a much smaller company, in financial terms, now than when it was before the Deepwater Horizon crisis.

Secondly, the CCI of 2010 created an adaptive psychological change in attitudes to innovation with investment levels in R&D subsequently declining. In 2010, BP's R&D Intensity stood at 0.26% and yet in the 14 financial years after the crisis, this figure had dropped to an average of 0.18% as the impact of multi-billion-dollar fines, clean-up, reparation and legal costs no doubt constrained the company's financial commitment to innovation-based investment.

Thirdly, a succession of CEOs have attempted to turnaround BP with a classic playbook that initially deployed strategies which cut costs and generated revenue through asset sales and divestments to raise the funds to cover the costs of the crisis and keep the company viable. The average tenure of the three CEOs following the crisis is considerably shorter than the average for S&P 500 CEOs, suggesting instability and a lack of a consistent long-term vision and ability to execute a cohesive strategy.

The Deepwater Horizon disaster created a Corporate Trauma with long-lasting psychological and financial consequences for BP. Despite attempts at strategic transformation and rebuilding stakeholder trust, the company continues to grapple with the legacy of the 2010 crisis and the lingering shadow that the Deepwater Horizon crisis casts over BP.

Wells Fargo & Company: America's Biggest Bank, America's Biggest Betrayal

Background

Wells Fargo has a rich and complex history dating back to 1852. Founded by Henry Wells and William Fargo, the company provided banking and express services for gold, mail, and other goods during the American West's Gold Rush of the mid-1800s. The Gold Rush sparked an enormous influx of people to California, dramatically altering its demographics and economy which resulted in the company expanding its operations to include stagecoach lines and the renowned Pony Express. Over time, the company's focus shifted, with banking operations separating from express services through numerous mergers and acquisitions. Wells Fargo grew into a major financial institution, and in 1998, it merged with Norwest Corporation in a multi-billion-dollar deal that created Wells Fargo & Company (WFC). Whilst the merger was structured such that Norwest acquired Wells Fargo, the combined company retained the Wells Fargo name due to its strong brand, iconic imagery and a reputation for reliability, stability and above all trust. The company cultivated an image of prudent management and had successfully navigated the worst effects of the Global Financial Crisis, unlike many of its peers, to deliver impressive returns.

However, as you will read in this case study, WFC's once trusted reputation has been severely damaged in recent years by a number of financial scandals that have led to a series of regulatory fines. In particular, the Consumer Financial Protection Bureau's (CFPB) US$185 million fine in 2016[1] is considered to be the crisis that triggered a critical downturn in the company's fortunes, even though WFC have also been hit by a subsequent fine of US$3 billion by the Department of Justice (DoJ) in 2020 for fraudulent banking practices[2]; and again in 2022 by the CFPB for US$3.7 billion for the mismanagement and intentionally deceptive practices relating to millions of customer auto loans, mortgages and deposit accounts.[3] These regulatory breaches led Rohit Chopra, CFPB Director, to state that the company was a "repeat offender" whose corporate behavior was a "rinse-repeat cycle of violating the law which has harmed millions of American families".[3] Wells Fargo & Company's reputation, previously built on the perception of strong customer service and ethical conduct, was crushed in the wake of significant negative media coverage and widespread public condemnation.

Today, WFC is among the 'Big Four' banks in the U.S., alongside JPMorgan Chase, Bank of America, and Citigroup with over four thousand domestic branches and consolidated assets of more than US$1.7 trillion.[1] The company is headquartered in San Francisco, California and operates in four market segments (Consumer Banking and Lending; Commercial Banking; Corporate and Investment Banking; and Wealth and Investment Management) which provides banking, investment, mortgage, and consumer and commercial finance products and services in both domestic and international markets. WFC's largest business unit, Consumer Banking and Lending is responsible for managing many of the day-to-day banking services of individuals and small businesses and consistently contributes to more than half of the company's annual revenue.[4]

A Corporate Crisis: The Trigger that Caused a Downward Spiral

In October 2013, a disgruntled WFC employee called the Los Angeles Times to complain that he and a number of co-workers had been fired from one of the company's suburban branches. The reason for the dismissals . . . creating unauthorized customer accounts and issuing debit or credit cards, sometimes through forged signatures.[5] The newspaper published an investigative report that detailed the pressure on employees to meet unrealistic sales goals and the resulting fraudulent activity. A company spokesperson acknowledged that 30 branch staff had been fired for being too focused on achieving sales targets and that their fraudulent behavior had compromised the company's ethical values. What appeared at the time to be a routine call to the Los Angeles Times, signaled the beginning of a more extensive regulatory investigation that became more widely known as the 'Wells Fargo fake accounts scandal'.

WFC's Critical Corporate Incident (CCI) occurred on the 8th September 2016, when the CFPB fined Wells Fargo Bank, a subsidiary of WFC, a total of US$185 million for "the widespread illegal practice of secretly opening unauthorized deposit and credit card accounts".[1] The CFPB said that the company had an overly aggressive sales culture that had driven employees to secretly open more than two million unauthorized deposit and credit card accounts without the consent of customers. These actions, which often resulted in unwarranted fees for customers, involved transferring funds from legitimate accounts to bogus customer accounts. WFC were ordered to fully compensate affected consumers and pay a fine of US$100 million to the CFPB's Civil Penalty Fund. Additional fines of US$85 million and US$50 million were paid to Los Angeles city and county authorities.

However, this wasn't the end of the case, and a further investigation by the DoJ resulted in a US$3 billion penalty on the 21st February 2020 relating to WFC's intentionally deceptive and criminal activity between 2002 and 2016. Initially, the fraud was exposed by the Los Angeles Times in 2013 and was considered to be an isolated incident. However, further investigations revealed that WFC staff had engaged in dishonesty and fraud on an industrial scale which led the company to fire 5,300 employees. The widespread deception was pervasive and led U.S. Attorney Andrew Murray (Western District, North Carolina) to comment that WFC's unlawful conduct was of "staggering size, scope and duration".[2] The DoJ investigation determined that WFC's 'Cross-sell Strategy', introduced after the 1998 merger with Norwest Corporation, employed a highly aggressive sales approach. The aim of this strategy was to increase sales volume and corporate growth by selling more financial products to existing customers. Moreover, while initially appearing successful, the new strategy resulted in a high-pressure, sales driven culture that made thousands of employees sell numerous products to existing customers, regardless of whether they needed them or not. The consequences of such a demanding working environment meant that employees resorted to a number of unlawful practices that included: identity theft, falsification of bank records, forged customer signatures, the creation of unauthorized PINs, transferring funds to unauthorized accounts, and altering customer contact information. All of which was an attempt to conceal the bank's fraudulent activities. It worked . . . for an unbelievable 14 years!

DoJ investigators also found that as early as 2002, senior managers at the Wells Fargo bank knew of the growing problem of unethical sales practices. Indeed, the bank's own investigations revealed that the issue was worsening, with warnings of a "growing plague" and a situation "spiraling out of control".[2] Despite these clear red flags and direct concerns about the sales strategy, the bank's leadership refused to accept that these occurrences were anything more than isolated incidents. U.S. Attorney Nick Hanna (Central District of California) summed up the criminal investigation saying that what had become widely known as 'The Wells Fargo fake accounts scandal' had demonstrated "a complete failure of leadership at multiple levels within the Bank. Simply put, Wells Fargo traded its hard-earned reputation for short-term profits, and harmed untold numbers of customers along the way".[2]

The once iconic brand had been built on a spirit of hope, adventure and boundless optimism that exemplified the California Gold Rush, and it established

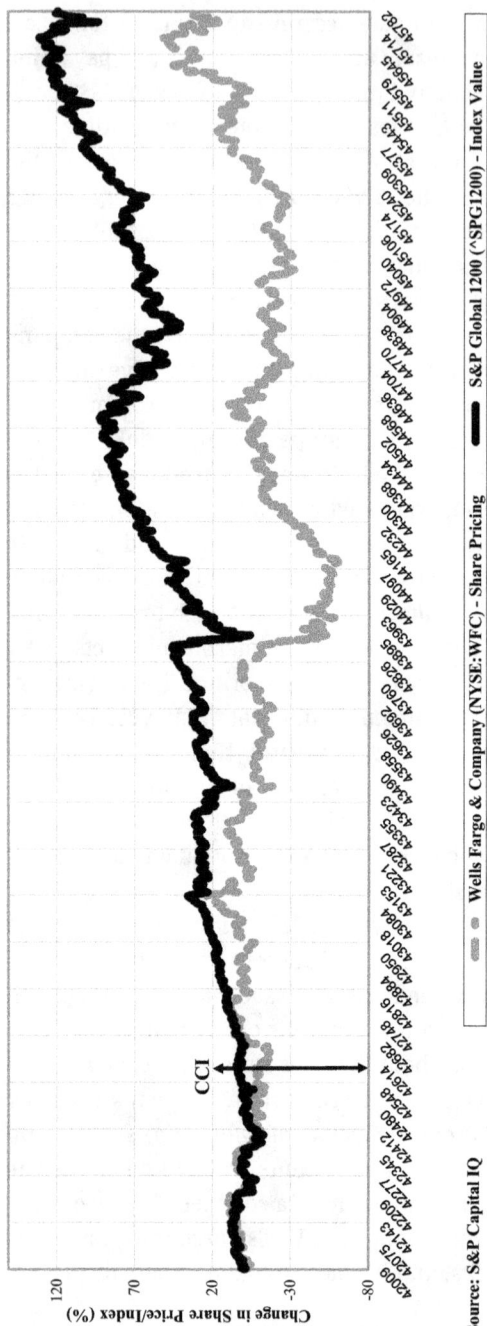

Source: S&P Capital IQ

Diagram 9: Share Price Performance of Wells Fargo & Co. v S&P Global 1200 Index (2015–2025).

a reputation for reliability, stability and trust in the ensuing years. Investors had previously viewed WFC as a "tightly run ship" [6] known for its efficient operations and low-risk profile which shielded it from economic shocks and major setbacks. In the aftermath of the fake accounts scandal, its reputation had been demolished by an intentional deception that stemmed from a deliberate decision to drive corporate profits with a strategy that aimed to increase annual sales at the expense of millions of customers.

The short-term effect on WFC's share price to the CFPB's US$185 million fine on the 8th September 2016, was negligible. Investors clearly regarded the penalty as no more than a 'slap on the wrist' by regulators as shares rose 13 cents, to US$49.90, at the close of trading that day.[6] However, market sentiment in WFC remained cautious in the face of what was considered to be a questionable organizational culture and an ongoing investigation by the DOJ into the fake accounts scandal. As a result, WFC shares traded at around US$46 in the four years prior to the US$3 billion fine in February 2020.[7] The longer-term consequences of the CCI, however, saw market sentiment turn against WFC as a result of a deliberate deception which had damaged investor trust and the company's credibility. A comparative analysis against leading companies, considered 'best-in-class', reveals a significant disparity in performance following the CCI. Having previously outperformed these firms between 2014 and most of 2016, WFC's share price has floundered since the date of the CCI, increasing by 48% compared to the S&P Global 1200 Index which has seen a substantial 110% growth in value[8] over the same time period (see Diagram 9). This underperformance of WFC's stock, relative to the broader market, suggests a pronounced negative impact of the CCI on investor confidence and indicates that WFC have failed to fully capitalize on the overall market's upward trajectory. From a Corporate Trauma perspective, this divergence in share price growth can be interpreted as a tangible, quantifiable physiological marker of a severe, triggered response.

An Adverse Modification in Corporate Culture

The word frequency analysis of innovation and risk words in annual reports over the period 2000 to 2024 provides an interesting illustration of how cultural attitudes at WFC have ebbed and flowed in relation to changes in organizational direction and business strategy (see Diagram 10 below). Following its acquisition by Norwest Corporation in 1998, WFC implemented an ambitious 'Cross-sell Strategy' that resulted in a rise in the use of innovation words between 2000 and 2004 and a decline of risk words. However, between 2005 and 2012 the use of innovation words consistently fell, whilst risk words remained higher in response to the economic uncertainty caused by the Global Financial Crisis. However, it is 2014 that is the most striking aspect of the cultural attitudes to innovation and risk at WFC, and in order to better understand what happened in 2014, the CEO statements in the annual reports between 2013 and 2015 have been analyzed and compared.

In 2013, Chairman and CEO John G. Stumpf's letter to shareholders presented WFC as a highly successful financial institution that was focused on customer service and building lasting relationships with customers by delivering sound business practices and responsible banking. The report also highlights the importance of rigorous risk management practices and maintaining strong controls to protect customers and the company. In 2015, Stumpf reinforced the company's commitment to building strong relationships with its stakeholders and delivering excellent customer service. However, the 2014 'blip' in the word frequency analysis of innovation and risk words is explained by Stumpf's emphasis on the company's commitment to its current culture and to the company's historical values. He stated that he believed "culture is the most important part of a company's success" and that in a single word, the WFC culture was all about "relationships" and that in serving its stakeholders the company had to "earn their trust" and "strive to do the right thing and act under the highest ethical standards of honesty, trust, and integrity".[9] At no point did Stumpf mention the Los Angeles Times report, nor the emerging inquiry by Federal regulators and the Los Angeles city attorney into the company's illegal practice of secretly opening unauthorized deposit and credit card accounts. Stumpf may have sensed the size and scale of an impending crisis, and instead of outlining WFC's innovation-based capabilities and strengths in risk management to shareholders, he doubled-down on an established culture that emphasized relationships, trust, and ethical conduct as cornerstones of the company's success.

Whilst the CFPB had imposed the largest regulatory fine in its history, investors and the market seemed to view it as merely symbolic, especially considering WFC's position as "the world's most valuable bank by market capitalization"[9] at US$242 billion. Nonetheless, as a psychological marker of Corporate Trauma, the word frequency analysis demonstrates that the Los Angeles Times report in 2013 acted as a pre-emptive warning of what was to come on the 8th September 2016 as it had created an adaptive change in WFC's cultural attitudes to innovation and risk in 2014. Interestingly, the word frequency analysis for the period 2016 to 2020 demonstrates a clear shift in cultural attitudes to innovation and risk, with a five-year decline in the use of risk words. This decline in attitudes to risk was reversed following the DoJ's multi-billion-dollar penalty in 2020 and the emergence of the COVID-19 global pandemic.

WFC

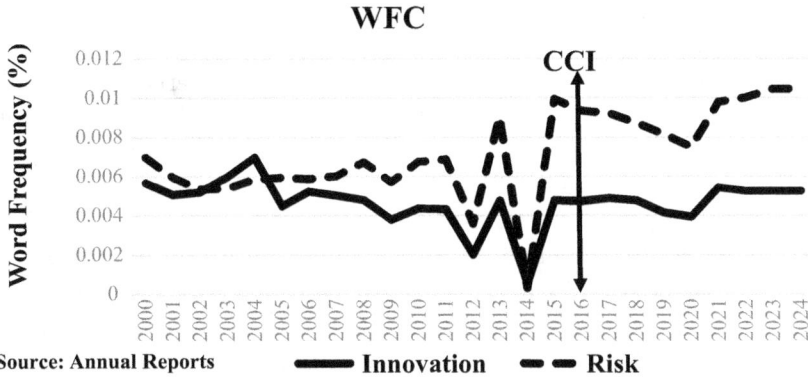

Diagram 10: Cultural Attitudes to Innovation and Risk (2000–2024).

Corporate Financial Performance

Undertaking a corporate financial analysis for WFC presents a dilemma. Having been described by regulators as a "repeat offender"[3] whose corporate behavior has harmed millions of its customers and resulted in numerous penalties amounting to billions of dollars, the key question is whether or not the financial data is valid and useable for analysis? The DoJ found that WFC had engaged in widespread illegal and fraudulent sales practices between 2002 and 2016 in an attempt to boost the company's revenues. This likely boosted operating income and inflated the company's financial performance, potentially attracting investors and overstating its market valuation. WFC, in contrast to numerous competitors, demonstrated remarkable resilience during the Global Financial Crisis, achieving strong returns . . . we now know how they did it!

In essence, the reliability of WFC's historical financial data is compromised and determining the company's true performance in the context of fraudulent activities that were found to be of "staggering size, scope and duration"[2] is problematic. As such, whilst the data for the period between 2002 and 2015 is available, the long-term trends in the financial metrics from 'before' the crisis will not be discussed due to concerns over their validity. Nevertheless, the discussion that now follows will focus on the data between 2016 and 2024 when the company had been subject to closer regulatory scrutiny, particularly from the CFPB who were strident in their call for improvements in the company's compliance programs and corporate governance. As you will see in Table 5 below, the average market capitalization of US$218,798 million in the eight years following the crisis, is 9% lower than in 2016 when WFC's market capitalization was US$241,702 million.

This suggests that the company has faced challenges in maintaining the confidence of investors post-crisis. Furthermore, the analysis highlights a concerning trend in the company's core financial performance, with a deterioration in both revenue and operating income between 2016 and 2024. Revenue has declined by 7%, indicating potential challenges in generating sales and more alarmingly, operating income has plummeted by 33%. This significant drop suggests that the company is experiencing substantial pressure on its profitability, potentially due to increased operating costs, reduced efficiency, and the impact of regulatory penalties. The financial analysis also raises important questions about WFC's long-term financial health and its ability to recover from the reputational and financial damage caused by its fraudulent sales practices.

Table 5: Wells Fargo & Co. Comparative Average Financial Performance (2000–2024).

Source: S&P Capital IQ	Pre-CCI Average (2000–2015)	Critical Corporate Incident (2016)	Post-CCI Average (2017–2024)	Change in Post CCI Average since 2016 (%)
Market Capitalization (US$ mn)	129,399	241,702	218,798	−9
Revenue (US$ mn)	50,690	84,541	78,300	−7
Operating Income (US$ mn)	20,363	34,480	23,112	−33

A Transgenerational Response Over Multiple Corporate Generations

CEO John G. Stumpf had overseen an aggressive, and fraudulent, sales culture that had boosted profits and the company's market capitalization through the darkest days of the Global Financial Crisis and beyond. The CFPB's regulatory fine on the 8th September 2016 resulted in Stumpf's resignation a month later, on the 12th October 2016, but not before appearing in front of the U.S. Congress where he stated that "he took responsibility for the problems, but would not admit that there was anything wrong with the bank's broader culture"[10]. Stumpf had been with the company for 34 years and had served as its CEO since 2007. For a senior executive who was named the Banker of the Year in 2013, it was a spectacular fall from grace.

Timothy J. Sloan was appointed as CEO on 13th October 2016, having previously served as WFC's President and Chief Operating Officer. With 29 years of experience in other roles within the company, outgoing CEO Stumpf commented that "I know no better individual to lead this company forward than Tim Sloan".[11] Sloan's tenure can be characterized as leading a company that was navigating a significant crisis and whose primary goal was to rebuild trust and transparency with a range of stakeholders with more frequent communication and a reform of the company that would eliminate sales goals and enhance governance mechanisms. In the immediate aftermath of the crisis, Sloan initiated efforts to "make things right" by complying with the regulatory enforcement requirements to refund fees, review customer accounts, and reaching out to affected customers. He emphasized the severity of the challenges posed by a widespread culture of "unacceptable sales practices" that had violated the company's core values and had resulted in a challenge that ranked "among the toughest in our company's history".[12] By 2017, Sloan's leadership shifted towards the transformational changes in culture, with a specific focus on ethics symbolized by a new streamlined 'Vision, Values & Goals' which had replaced the previous "37 page expression of [the company's] culture"[13]. There was also a strong emphasis on strengthening governance and risk management, including the creation of an Office of Ethics, Oversight and Integrity. Sloan expressed optimism, asserting that the transformational changes at the company will make "Wells Fargo over time not just *a* leader but *the* financial services leader".[13] However, Sloan's tenure was suddenly cut short when he resigned on 28th March 2019 after an investigation by The New York Times revealed that "Wells Fargo workers say they remain under heavy pressure to squeeze extra money out of customers. Some have witnessed colleagues bending or breaking internal rules to meet ambitious performance goals".[14] The U.S. Congress called for Sloan's resignation as he had effectively become a "a lightning rod for criticism"[15] by being too closely linked to a series of fraudulent scandals and a deceitful corporate culture. While he stressed the company's underlying financial strength, WFC's financial performance over Sloan's tenure saw revenue stagnate and operating income decline by 17% between 2016 and 2018.

C. Allen Parker was appointed as CEO, on an interim basis, on the 28th March 2019. Having served as the company's General Council since 2017, his corporate governance experience and good relationship with regulators provided WFC with the necessary breathing space to find a suitable and permanent replacement. His tenure lasted 7 months.

Charles Scharf became CEO on the 21st October 2019. His "strong track record in initiating and leading change"[16] and extensive senior executive experience at the Bank of New York Mellon, Visa Inc., JP Morgan Chase and Citigroup would provide wider industry insights and an ability to challenge existing assumptions and drive cultural change. His appointment, as a respected external leader, aimed to boost investor confidence and improve the company's reputation. His tenure as CEO continues to date.

At the start of Scharf's tenure he acknowledged the company's past failures and a flawed operating model that breached customer trust. He also emphasized the need to rectify these issues to regain stakeholder trust, including customers, employees, regulators, and shareholders. It was a recurring narrative for a company described as a "repeat offender" by regulators. Whilst the reputational cost of the 'fake accounts scandal' was significant, Scharf also commented that the company's financial results "were not as strong as we aspire them to be" as a result of litigation and customer remediation costs; and that now was the time to "fully capture the opportunity to once again be one of the most respected and successful banks in the country".[17] Furthermore, Scharf intended to simplify the company's operations by selling, downsizing and curtailing non-core businesses. This classic turnaround play, however, has to date, failed to improve the company's financial performance during Scharf's tenure. In 2019, revenue was US$84,227 million and by 2024 it had fallen 7% to US$77,962 million; operating income also fell by 8%, from US$25,967 million to US$23,897 million over the same period. Given this sluggish financial performance, it is no surprise that market capitalization has only improved by 2%, from US$227,016 million to US$231,015 million between 2019 and 2024.

A persistent issue that Scharf has faced during his tenure is WFC's problematic culture. In 2019 he aimed to overhaul the company's culture and strengthen its risk management policies and processes in order to meet regulatory expectations and compliance. However, two years into his tenure, he commented that WFC had been "too slow in building and implementing appropriate risk and control frameworks" and "too slow in addressing legacy issues".[18]

Fast forward to 2024 and the importance of cultural change continues to dominate WFC's corporate psyche. Scharf commented that the company had undergone a fundamental transformation, re-setting priorities and restructuring management. Since 2019, the Operating Committee had been completely revitalized with every person "either new to the company or new to their role"[19] in order to critically re-evaluate legacy strategies and lead on substantial changes in the company and its operations. Significantly, the legacy of the 2016 crisis continued to cast a shadow over the company, however, Scharf advised shareholders that "regulators have closed 10 consent orders since 2019, including one in 2024 and four in early 2025"[19] relating to its previous illegal sales practices. This marked a crucial milestone in WFC's rehabilitation and provided the company with an important opportunity to move forward.

In essence, a succession of CEOs have endeavored to turnaround a company burdened by a toxic sales culture that fueled WFC's growth under Stumpf's leadership. The company's Cross-sell Strategy ultimately crumbled under the weight of regulatory scrutiny and the long-term consequences of prioritizing short-term gains over legal and ethical conduct revealed a cultural flaw that Stumpf had refused to admit. Changing a path dependent culture that was deeply entrenched in aggressive sales targets has been problematic, despite increased regulatory scrutiny and repeated leadership changes. Sloan's tenure was framed as a continuation of the old guard and his efforts to transform the company's culture, despite initiatives like streamlining the company's values and strengthening governance, proved to be insufficient. The lingering trauma of the 'fake accounts scandal' and continued reports of pressure on employees to meet unrealistic sales goals ultimately led to his resignation. Scharf's arrival signaled a shift towards external expertise and a more decisive approach to cultural change. He openly acknowledged the company's past failures and committed to rebuilding trust. However, despite efforts to streamline operations and strengthen risk management, the company's financial performance remained stagnant. Scharf's continued emphasis on cultural transformation and rebuilding investor trust highlighted the persistent nature of a problem that he and previous incumbents' had inherited. Even in 2025, the company was still addressing legacy issues relating to a scandal that was initially exposed in 2013. The long-term consequences of the scandal has resulted in an average tenure of CEOs Sloan, Parker and Stumpf at Wells Fargo of just 2.67 years, which again, is unusually short when compared to the S&P 500 average of 9.3 years. Successive CEOs have been unable to turnaround WFC's culture, which is indicative of a systemic cultural problem, not just individual leadership failures. That problem was revealed by the crisis in 2016 and resultant Corporate Trauma.

Conclusions

The Wells Fargo & Company case study presents a cautionary tale of a once-revered institution's dramatic fall from grace, driven by a toxic culture and a relentless pursuit of profit at the expense of ethical conduct and customer trust. What began as a local news report of unethical sales practices spiraled into a national crisis, culminating in massive regulatory fines and a damaged reputation. The root of the problem lay in a Cross-sell Strategy implemented after the 1998 merger, which fostered an aggressive sales culture that incentivized employees to engage in fraudulent activities and management to prioritize short-term gains over ethical conduct. The evidence presented in this case provides support for a number of conclusions that substantiates the argument that the WFC are suffering from a number of adaptive physiological and psychological effects that are indicative of a company suffering from Corporate Trauma.

Firstly, the physiological financial markers demonstrate that WFC's long-term share price performance, when compared to best-in-class benchmarks, has consistently underperformed since the CCI almost a decade ago. It's a clear sign of enduring trauma. Furthermore, the corporate financial analysis reveals a clear deterioration in WFC's performance post-crisis, with declines in market capitalization, revenue, and operating income. This data underscores the profound impact of the fraudulent activities on the company's long-term financial health.

Secondly, the 2013 Los Angeles Times investigative report, and the subsequent regulatory inquiry, foreshadowed the CCI in 2016. It prompted WFC to double-down on its communications to shareholders and re-enforce the message that its corporate culture promoted values of trust, honesty and integrity. The muted response, a slight increase in share price, from shareholders to the regulatory fine in 2016, suggests that investors were not immediately concerned about the long-term implications of the penalty. The market at that time viewed the regulators' actions as no more than a 'slap on the wrist' for the world's biggest bank. However, the subsequent five-year decline in the use of risk-related words could plausibly be seen as an indication of complacency within the company, suggesting the belief within WFC that they had escaped serious repercussions. They had effectively dodged a bullet.

Thirdly, chronic corporate financial performance and an average tenure shorter than one would expect at an S&P 500 company are clear indicators that successive CEOs have struggled to implement the classic turnaround playbook of cost-cutting, restructuring, asset sales, and re-focusing the company on core business. The subsequent leadership transitions, from Sloan to Parker to Scharf, were marked by attempts to rectify the damage of the crisis and rebuild trust. However, the persistent emphasis on cultural transformation highlights the inherited and transgenerational nature of the problem. The unusually short tenures of recent CEOs is a manifestation of a deeply flawed corporate culture that continues to plague WFC. CEO John Stumpf's denial of a collective cultural problem, even in the face of mounting evidence, underscored the company's deep-seated resistance to change.

The Director of the CFPB delivered a scathing indictment of Wells Fargo & Company, labeling it a "repeat offender" with a corporate culture characterized by a "rinse-repeat cycle of violating the law".[3] This pattern of misconduct, according to the CFPB, had inflicted significant harm upon millions of American families, highlighting a general failure of compliance and ethical conduct. Wells Fargo & Company was once America's biggest bank, and yet, it will be forever remembered for committing America's biggest betrayal of its customers.

Volkswagen AG: Cheat to Compete

Background

It's the perfect storm. An existential storm. Volkswagen AG (VW) is navigating a complex landscape and a number of significant hurdles as it grapples with intense competition from both established electric vehicle (EV) competitors like Tesla and rapidly emerging Chinese EV players. This, coupled with the substantial economic strain of transitioning away from traditional combustion engines at a time of slower-than-expected EV sales across the industry is creating a challenging competitive environment for VW.

On the global stage China has emerged as an increasingly dominant force in the global EV market. Leading Chinese EV producers like BYD, Geely, Nio, and SAIC Motor have benefitted from strong government support, a robust domestic market, investments in innovative technologies and supply chain control that have provided these players with a substantial competitive cost advantage. Furthermore, U.S. President Donald Trump's significant increase in auto import tariffs will no doubt drastically impact the competitiveness of all European car manufacturers in the U.S. market. In Europe, economic growth has slowed and even stagnated in some countries due to high inflation, rising energy prices, and the geopolitical uncertainty caused by the Russia-Ukraine War. In particular, Germany, traditionally the economic powerhouse of Europe has experienced a contraction in its economy in 2023 and 2024, and the outlook for the future has been described as "uncertain".[1] A number of cyclical and structural challenges were responsible for this poor economic performance which included: Russian energy dependence and resulting energy price increases; a reliance on exports at a time of weakening global demand for its (largely) industrial products; the costs of accelerating the transition to renewable energy infrastructure; and the uncertainty for business caused by recent federal elections and the new coalition government. For VW it's not only the perfect storm, it could also be an existential storm.

VW has long been regarded as a company that symbolizes Germany's remarkable recovery and industrial resurgence after World War II. "Wirtschaftswunder" (i.e. economic miracle) is a widely used term to describe the nation's and VW's engineering excellence, operational efficiency and its global expansion over recent decades. In the 1930s, Adolf Hitler sought to create an affordable 'people's car' (i.e. Volkswagen) to boost the German automotive industry and provide transportation for the masses. The result was the iconic Beetle, known for its distinctive rounded shape and air-cooled engine. As VW grew, further renowned brands were added to the passenger car portfolio which catered for the mass (e.g. Skoda, SEAT), premium (e.g. Audi, Porche) and luxury (e.g. Bentley, Bugatti, Lamborghini) markets, whilst also competing in Commercial Vehicles, Power Engineering and Financial Services markets.

However, by 2024, the economic miracle had turned into an economic nightmare. VW is currently facing a number of strategic challenges with the transition to EVs that include the rising costs of production in Germany and fierce competition from lower-cost Chinese manufacturers. A "drop of 64% in third quarter profits in 2024"[2] illustrates the scale of the impact on VW's business. The management's response, a classic turnaround play – cut costs to stabilize the company and ensure its future financial viability. In October 2024, VW announced plans to restructure the workforce that would see the closure of at least three factories and thousands of employees out of work. Daniela Cavallo, head of VW's powerful works council, has called her battle with management "existential"[3] for the group's 296,000 Germany-based workers. The perfect storm continues to rage.

A Corporate Crisis: The Trigger that Caused a Downward Spiral

The seeds of VW's Corporate Trauma were sown by a Critical Corporate Incident (CCI) which occurred on the 18th September 2015, when the United States Environmental Protection Agency (EPA) issued the company with a Notice of Violation of the Clean Air Act. The EPA alleged that the company had sold approximately 590,000 diesel vehicles in the United States (model years 2009 to 2016) which contained a high-tech computer software algorithm known as a "defeat device"[4]. Intended to deceive, the device was "designed to cheat on federal emissions tests"[4] and was activated solely during federal emissions testing, thus masking nitrogen oxide emissions that were up to 40 times the legal limit under typical driving conditions.

The immediate effects of the crisis saw VW shares fall by 19% on the day of the EPA announcement and 17% the day after[5] wiping billions of euros from the company's market capitalization. On the 22nd September 2015 VW admitted that the deception had occurred on a global scale with the defeat software having been fitted in 11 million vehicles worldwide. The following day, CEO Martin Winterkorn resigned saying that he was "shocked" and "not aware of any wrongdoing" and that he was "clearing the way"[6] for a fresh start for the company. The EPA issued two further violation notices of the Clean Air Act in November 2015 and January 2016 against Volkswagen, Audi, and Porsche.

The VW emissions scandal became known as "Dieselgate" and the once iconic brand was now considered to be just as toxic as the poisonous emissions discharged from its vehicles. The company's internal investigations subsequently found that the intentionally deceptive fraud stemmed from a decision in 2005 to

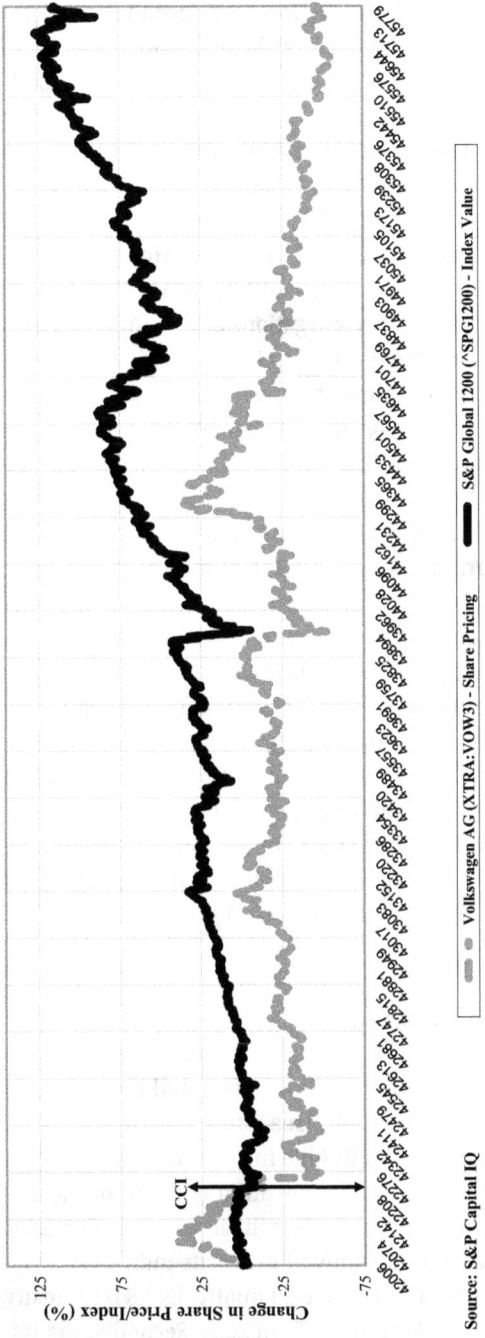

Source: S&P Capital IQ

Diagram 11: Share Price Performance of VW v S&P Global 1200 Index (2015–2025).

aggressively market diesel cars in the United States. However, faced with stricter emissions standards for nitrogen oxides compared to those in Europe, a small group of VW employees chose to install the defeat device in order to meet their budget and timeline.[7]

The longer-term consequences of the CCI are, however, more substantial. On the 28th June 2016 the company entered into a series of multi-billion-dollar settlements to resolve the fraud and on the 11th January 2017, VW agreed to pay a US$2.8 billion criminal penalty and US$1.5 billion to cover civil penalties[4]. However, the financial penalties didn't end there. The company agreed with the U.S. Federal Trade Commission to spend up to US$14.7 billion to settle allegations of cheating emissions tests and deceiving customers by offering them a buyback and lease termination, and to mitigate the pollution from these vehicles by investing in green vehicle technology.[8] Ultimately, the scale of a deception with global reach is reported to have cost the company over US$34 billion[9] in fines and legal costs, making it the largest automotive industry scandal in history.

The longer-term consequences of the CCI also meant that market sentiment also turned against VW. With their corporate reputation in ruins as a result of an 'intentional' deception, the company suffered a catastrophic collapse in stakeholder trust, falling sales, reduced brand loyalty and diminished purchase intentions for VW vehicles. While VW's share price outperformed 'best-in-class' companies during most of 2015, the crisis resulted in a loss of credibility and trust with investors which has seen its share price subsequently fall by 40% since the date of the CCI, at a time when the share price of firms in the S&P Global 1200 Index had increased by 127%[10] (see Diagram 11). From a Corporate Trauma perspective, this is a clear physiological marker that reflects a severe response 'triggered' by the CCI on the 18th September 2015. In a single moment, VW's image plummeted from an iconic brand to into a symbol of corporate criminality.

An Adverse Modification in Corporate Culture

Diagram 12 below illustrates a frequency analysis of innovation and risk words in annual reports over the period 2000 to 2024 – and three issues clearly stand out. Firstly, the effects of the bursting of the Dot.com Bubble in 2000 undoubtedly produced a decline in VW's cultural attitudes toward innovation and rise in the frequency use of risk words. However, this effect was short lived and between 2001 and 2005 there was a sharp rise in the use of innovation words indicating VW's cultural orientation to stay relevant in the marketplace. Equally, its R&D Intensity during this period increased from 2.9% in 2001 to 4.34% in 2005. Secondly, the impact of the Global Financial Crisis dented the company's cultural orientation toward innovation in 2007, although its long-term commitment to investing in a pipeline of patents and innovative products to boost productivity and growth was demonstrated with R&D Intensity figures of 4.89% in 2007 and 4.48% in 2008. However, the third and most striking feature of the word frequency analysis is VW's adaptive, and negative, cultural response to the CCI in 2015. The long-term consequences of the crisis has seen a sharp decline in the use of innovation words and an increase in the use of risk words. Whilst VW have continued to invest in R&D projects related to EV transition, with an average R&D Intensity figure of 5.16% in the 9 years following the CCI, they are 'communicating' a sense of risk aversion in annual reports that will no doubt have negatively affected both investor and wider stakeholder confidence in their ability to make a full and successful transition to the EV market. As a psychological marker of Corporate Trauma, there is clear evidence to suggest that the CCI of 2015 has triggered an adaptive change in cultural attitudes toward risk aversion which is most likely damaging VW's health, development and long-term growth.

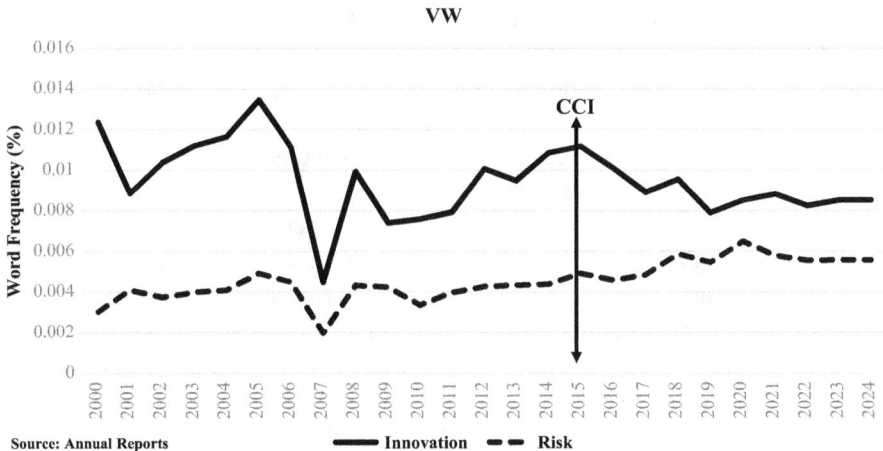

Diagram 12: Cultural Attitudes to Innovation and Risk (2000–2024).

Corporate Financial Performance

Unlike the other companies presented in this chapter, VW has shown a remarkable level of financial resilience in the wake of the Dieselgate scandal. The analysis of VW's share price performance against the S&P Global 1200 Index demonstrates a long-term and strategic drift against best-in-class companies since the date of the CCI. However, setting aside this comparative analysis, Table 6 below illustrates that the key physiological markers of the Corporate Trauma from 'before and after' the CCI in 2015 are *'not'* present. At face value, it's an interesting dilemma for the argument of Corporate Trauma! Having said that, VW's financial resilience can be explained as follows.

With an average market capitalization of €76,246 million in the 9 years following the crisis, this figure is 72% higher than the average market capitalization of €44,369 million over the period 2000 to 2014. Conversely, in the four years that followed the crisis, the company's market capitalization dropped from €69,130 million in 2015 to €53,156 million by 2019 as VW's orchestrated fraud had undermined the credibility of its brand reputation and betrayed investor trust. Interestingly, 2020 saw a considerable uplift in VW's market capitalization to €121,531 million following a surge in investor enthusiasm for the company's aggressive plans to push into the EV market. The 'NEW AUTO' strategy aimed to position VW in the "world of mobility in 2030" whilst making the company more "efficient, innovative, customer-oriented and sustainable, and systematically gearing it toward profitable growth"[11]. The strategy included plans for battery production and infrastructure which investors saw as an indication that VW had put its troubles behind them and were now back on track to becoming a serious contender in the rapidly growing EV market. Furthermore, the general recovery of the global economy, after the initial shock of the COVID-19 pandemic, also saw a general rise in market confidence which also contributed to the upward momentum of VW's share price. In essence, the combination of a compelling EV strategy, favorable market sentiment, and positive financial performance drove a significant increase in VW's market capitalization. Investor sentiment in the company, however, could not be maintained in the face of the rising costs, increasing debt, structural workforce changes, union unrest, and the increasingly formidable EV competitors from China. By 2024, the company's value had fallen by 54% from its peak in 2021 to €55,811 million.

The revenue performance from 'before and after' the CCI also provides another illustration of VW's resilience and ability to generate sales. Between 2000 and 2014, the company's average revenue amounted to €123,117 million, compared to a post crisis average of €259,395 million between 2016 and 2024. This impressive level of revenue growth is equally matched by a significant increase in operating income where the change in the pre-and post-CCI average is a remarkable 227%. This performance can largely be explained by VW's global expansion, particularly in markets like China, which has been a major driver of revenue growth. Furthermore, the company's market development strategy saw WW enter a wide range of customer segments that included mass, premium and luxury brands which has helped to mitigate the risks associated with the effect of global economic cycles on individual market segments. In addition, the company introduced restructuring and cost-cutting measures following the crisis in 2015 which significantly improved its operating income.

In many ways, this classic turnaround playbook has worked for VW, however, the financial performance looks very different when we examine the same financial variables post the crisis in 2015. The 'Change in Post CCI Average since 2015' indicates that average market capitalization increased by 10%, average revenue by 22% and average operating income by 162%.

Table 6: VW Comparative Average Financial Performance (2000–2024).

Source: S&P Capital IQ	Pre-CCI Average (2000–2014)	Critical Corporate Incident (2015)	Post-CCI Average (2016–2024)	Change in Post CCI Average since 2015 (%)
Market Capitalization (€ mn)	44,369	69,130	76,246	10
Revenue (€ mn)	123,117	213,292	259,395	22
Operating Income (€ mn)	5,600	6,998	18,319	162

A Transgenerational Response Over Multiple Corporate Generations

After the resignation of CEO Martin Winterkorn in the wake of the 'Dieselgate' scandal, VW's Supervisory Board announced the immediate appointment of Matthias Müller as CEO on the 25th September 2015. Müller, a highly experienced automotive executive and Chairman at Porsche AG, was seen as someone who was "of great strategic, entrepreneurial and social competence".[12] Müller's tenure can be characterized by one corporate objective . . . winning back the trust of investors and customers. He immediately apologized to shareholders for the "irregularities relating to diesel engines"[13] and for the trust that had been broken. Recognizing the loss of credibility in the brand, he committed to a comprehensive overhaul of VW's corporate culture and values, prioritizing integrity, transparency, and responsibility as cornerstones. Müller also believed that VW would emerge from the crisis stronger than before and that the new 'Strategy 2025' would transform the company by adapting to the changing market demands for e-mobility and new mobility services. Notwithstanding the crisis, VW's financial performance during Müller's tenure was solid, driven by cost-cutting measures that focused on dropping some planned investments and eliminating nonessential expenditures such as management performance bonuses. As a result, operating income increased from €6,998 million in 2015 to €15,086 million in 2017. A significant accomplishment. However, while revenue had increased by only 8% over the same period, investor sentiment was more guarded as the company moved through a damaging litigation process where the sheer scale of the deception, reaching across the globe, amounted to tens of billions of dollars in fines and legal costs. Despite being given a contract until February 2020, the Board of Management and Supervisory Board fired Müller on the 10th April 2018 in an attempt to "move past the lingering effects of its 2015 diesel emissions scandal"[14]. Although Mueller was not directly implicated in the emissions rigging, his leadership faced scrutiny in Germany, with many believing he and other executives were insufficiently responsive as the scandal unfolded.

Herbert Diess, VW's brand chief, was appointed as CEO on the 12th April 2018 in a management shake-up that was designed to aggressively drive forward VW's transition to the EV market. Diess aimed to revolutionize VW, transitioning the traditional automaker into a global leader in sustainable mobility. His strategy, 'NEW AUTO' centered on three key pillars: digitalization, electrification, and boosting shareholder value through significantly increased dividends – all of which intended to transform the company.[15] He oversaw the launch of VW's dedicated electric vehicle platform and committed €47 billion for e-mobility and digitalization, alongside implementing significant cost-cutting measures.[16] Diess's tenure was exemplified by a period of intense corporate transformation, and his commitment to delivering value to shareholders through dividend increases had improved VW's market capitalization by 27% between 2018 and 2021. This notable outcome was not matched, however, by the revenue and operating income results, which had only increased by 6% and 8% respectively over the same period.

The specter of the emissions scandal returned once again in 2019, when Deiss and three other VW executives were charged with market manipulation in connection with 'Dieselgate'. These executives were accused of delaying the disclosure of the emissions scandal's financial impact to investors, which slowed down crucial warnings to vehicle owners and authorities in Europe and the US. However the charges were dropped when VW agreed to pay a fine of €9 million.[17,18] Controversy was never too far from Deiss having been criticized only months earlier for using the phrase *'Ebit macht frei'* (EBIT makes you free) at a company event. This expression closely resembled the Nazi slogan *'Arbeit macht frei'* (work sets you free) found at concentration camp gates, and whilst he claimed that he didn't intend to use rhetoric reminiscent of Nazi propaganda, he apologized for the "unfortunate choice of words"[19] when referring to VW's recent profits. Questions over Diess's management style, a tendency for comparing VW unfavorably to Tesla, a plan to cut 30,000 jobs in Germany as part of a cost management and productivity plan, the resultant union backlash, and problems with a major software technology project created a sense of instability at the company.[20] Diess's leadership cast a shadow over VW and uncertainty over his future resulted in the company's market value falling from a high of €121,531 million in 2020 to €76,155 million by the time he resigned on the 30th July 2022.

Oliver Blume took over as CEO on the 1st September 2022, while continuing to lead Porsche AG. At the time of his appointment Blume said that his dual leadership role would be temporary, nevertheless, he remains in charge almost three years later arguing that maintaining both roles enables him to better direct the restructuring and cost-cutting initiatives required to strengthen the group's finances during a time of market turbulence. Dissatisfied investors have openly questioned his capacity to deal with the demands of both positions amid a structural industry change that had led to the company to issue a profit warning and announce 35,000 job losses.[21] As a result of negative investor sentiment, VW's market capitalization during Blume's tenure has fallen by 27% and operating income has declined by 17% between 2022 and 2024, even though revenues increased by 16% over the same period.

To date, Blume's tenure has been defined by a company that remains in transition. VW, like many other legacy auto manufacturers, faces a complex balancing act in navigating the switch to electric vehicles while still serving the needs of customers to continue to offer more affordable combustion engine vehicles. Blume has recognized the variable pace of EV adoption globally and the need for a phased approach to transition, with VW continuing to produce combustion, hybrid and electric vehicles, at least in the short-term. There is no doubt that regulatory $CO2$ emission requirements will continue to frame Blume's objective to position VW as a 'Global Automotive Tech Driver' and whilst the company have set clear targets for growth, transitioning to an electric future will come at a significant financial cost. The planned workforce reductions are forecast to save €1.5 billion per year until 2030, and the development of the product range has resulted in an average annual R&D investment, between 2016 and 2024, of €13,350 million. Interestingly, the costs of the Dieselgate scandal and transition to electric vehicles has seen a dramatic change in the Volkswagen Group's capital structure, with debt levels increasing from €145,605 million in 2015 to the post crisis level of €255,537 million in 2024. Whilst investors are likely to view this significant increase in debt as a necessary strategic effort to finance long-term growth initiatives, they may also see this as a move that increases their levels of financial risk as VW is committed to making fixed interest payments at a time when its ability to produce a profit is under pressure.

The impact of high CEO turnover on VW has brought a level of strategic inconsistency with each new executive bringing a different approach and potentially disrupting ongoing initiatives and creating confusion. The average tenure of VW's three CEOs since the crisis in 2015 is just 3 years, which is remarkably short when compared to the S&P 500 average. Successive CEOs have been unable to turnaround VW's culture which is indicative of a deep-seated Corporate Trauma caused by the crisis in 2015, and the compounding effects of an industry in transition, regulatory requirements, and agile new EV competitors.

Conclusions

Trauma in humans can manifest in a wide range of physical and psychological signs and symptoms which can vary significantly from person to person and appear immediately after a traumatic event, or they may emerge months or even years later. As such, the signs of trauma are not always clear-cut as they can manifest in a wide variety of ways, making them difficult to identify. Just like individuals with PTSD, the evidence presented on VW has shown that the Dieselgate scandal was a pivotal moment, causing a severe shock to VW's reputation. In addition, there are a number of dysfunctional adaptive physiological and psychological changes which are indicative of a company in distress, whilst at the same time, VW have also demonstrated a remarkable level of financial resilience. As such, the evidence presented above provides the underpinning for a number of conclusions that offers a more nuanced view of Corporate Trauma.

Firstly, the physiological financial markers demonstrate that VW's long-term share price performance, when compared to best-in-class benchmarks, has consistently underperformed since the CCI almost a decade ago. It's a clear sign of enduring trauma. However, VW's corporate financial performance demonstrated a short-term decline in the immediate aftermath of the crisis, but a considerable turnaround in its fortunes, driven by a global expansion strategy spearheaded by the opportunities in the Chinese market.

Secondly, the CCI of 2015 created an adaptive psychological change and lasting impact on VW's culture. It triggered a clear shift towards risk aversion, evidenced by a sharp decline in 'innovation' words and a corresponding increase in 'risk' words in annual reports. Despite the shift towards risk aversion, VW continued to invest in R&D, particularly in EV technology. However, the language used in annual reports suggests a disconnect between actual R&D investment and the company's communicated cultural outlook. Essentially, VW are investing in innovation but talking about risk. The communicated risk aversion is likely to negatively affect investor and wider stakeholder confidence in VW's ability to successfully transition to the EV market.

Thirdly, a succession of CEOs have attempted to turnaround VW with the classic playbook of deploying strategies that include cost-cutting, restructuring, asset sales, and re-focusing the company on core business. However, the lingering effects of the Dieselgate scandal have persisted and been inherited through multiple CEO tenures, indicating a transgenerational impact that has created a number of adaptive changes which include: a damaged corporate reputation, a lack of investor confidence, and an organizational culture that has become more risk averse. It is no wonder that the average CEO tenure after the crisis event has been significantly less than the average CEO tenure across the S&P500. In his letter to shareholders in the 2024 annual report, CEO Oliver Blume, said that "the power of the Volkswagen Group lies in the power of our brands".[21] Regrettably, the Dieselgate scandal has severely undermined this assertion, transforming the company's public image from that of a once respected brand to one associated with corporate criminality.

Chapter 6
The Corporate Trauma Playbook

First things first . . . the classic turnaround playbook works! It's a proven method that has been used successfully by many companies to stabilize a dire financial situation and refocus their business on core strengths and areas of future profitability. A successful turnaround will usually see a failing firm emerge with a clearer sense of purpose and a stronger foundation for future growth. However, the lingering consequences of a past crisis can result in a deep-seated aversion to risk in organizations where the primary goal of strategic choices, policies and operational procedures is the avoidance, or minimization, of exposure to uncertain outcomes that could potentially lead to losses. It's the beginning of a downward spiral that can lead to missed opportunities for innovation, making the organization less adaptable to changing market conditions. Slower growth, lower profitability and subsequently less cash to invest in R&D and marketing can lead to a competitive disadvantage as other companies embrace innovation and new market opportunities more readily. A subsequent decline in performance often leads to an outflow of highly skilled employees and a decrease in the ambition and drive of those who remain. The CEO is fired. A new CEO is appointed, who uses the classic turnaround playbook . . . which may well fail. Part of the problem is that too many organizations consider the classic turnaround playbook as a panacea, blindly following a phased approach to recovery without *'accurately'* diagnosing the cause of chronic corporate underperformance.

At the beginning of this book, an important question was asked. What is the playbook for an organization who has appointed numerous new CEOs to turnaround a struggling business, but ultimately failed? The case studies presented in Chapter 5 will have given you a sense of how companies with a history of persistent underperformance and unsuccessful turnaround attempts could be suffering from an alternative diagnosis; a stress reaction to a previous crisis that has produced a hidden trauma which is inherited by successive CEOs attempting to turnaround the organization. These case studies also underscored the need for a *'new playbook'* and one that considers the unique challenges faced by companies that are grappling with the aftermath of a significant and historic crisis which created a trauma that continually hinders their ability to recover. As such, the Corporate Trauma Playbook argues that serial failed turnaround cases need a new approach and one that emphasizes the importance of historical insight, where executive leaders can pinpoint the foundational event that triggered the organization's trauma and its subsequent chronic underperformance. This understanding will enable them to identify and address the ingrained detrimental mindsets, actions, and dys-

https://doi.org/10.1515/9783111571126-006

functional cultural practices that have fueled the organization's deterioration and impeded its previous turnaround efforts. The Corporate Trauma Playbook offers a path out of the maze of uncertainty with a holistic approach that encompasses trauma acknowledgment, strategic renewal, sustained cultural transformation and rebuilding trust with stakeholders. As with all strategic playbooks, the following discussion will present a structured and phased approach to guide the turnaround process for organizations suffering from trauma and chronic underperformance.

Phase 1: Trauma Assessment and Diagnosis

Rationale: In order to gain a multi-faceted and nuanced understanding of the short-term effects and long-term consequences resulting from a crisis, the specific event that 'triggered' the downturn in the performance of an organization needs to be identified. This reference point is crucial for providing context, enabling meaningful comparisons, and facilitating effective analysis and decision-making. Without a clear reference point, data and information can be ambiguous, lack perspective, and fail to drive insightful conclusions and corrective actions. Once the crisis event has been identified, an analysis of a range of financial and non-financial metrics needs to be undertaken, and importantly, these should assess performance from 'before and after' the crisis. The time frame for 'before' the crisis will be dependent on each organization's circumstances.

Actionable Tactics

Undertake a Root Cause Analysis: Identify the specific event or crisis that triggered the organization's decline. As we have seen in the case studies in Chapter 5, some of these incidents are obvious and will be easy to identify (e.g. regulatory fine, product recall, cybersecurity attack, environmental disaster) whilst others may be slow-burn crises that are less evident at first (e.g. an investor call, small ethical lapses, a customer complaint) but can be particularly dangerous because they might not trigger immediate alarm or decisive action until significant damage has already occurred.

Conduct a Financial Performance Analysis: Undertake an analysis of the company's share price (assuming it has one) and benchmark it against its 'competitive set' and wider stock market indices (e.g. S&P Global 1200, NASDAQ, FTSE 100) to assess investor sentiment. Supplement this analysis with a comparison of financial data that compares a range of appropriate metrics. The case studies in Chapter 5 used market capitalization, revenue, operating income and R&D spend, however, more specific metrics related to the company and industry may be more appropriate (e.g. *Occupancy Rate* for hotels, *Cost of Goods Sold* for manufacturers, *Same-Store Sales Growth* for retailers).

Conduct a Non-Financial Performance Analysis: Non-financial metrics are referred to as business drivers because they are seen as leading indicators that influence future financial performance. These metrics are diverse, and again, company or industry specific so think of this analysis in terms of generating a 'Balanced Scorecard' where metrics such as customer churn, staff turnover, staff absenteeism, and sentiment from investors, media, and regulators – will provide a comprehensive view that complements the financial analysis.

Carry out a Leadership and Governance Analysis: Assessing the impact of a crisis on executive leadership is easy to identify. We have seen this in the case studies presented in Chapter 5 where a succession of CEOs have attempted to turnaround each company, however, the rapid turnover at the top has resulted in organizational instability, an inconsistent long-term vision and difficulties in executing a successful turnaround strategy. The key metric to use is *CEO tenure* benchmarked against the average CEO tenure in S&P 500 of 9.3 years.

A corporate crisis often acts as a catalyst for significant changes in a company's approach to risk management. As we have seen in the case studies, each crisis triggered an adaptive cultural change in attitudes to innovation and risk which was communicated in each company's annual report to shareholders. This increased risk aversion will, however, become deeply embedded in revised governance policies, which aim to create a more resilient, ethical, and sustainable organization by prioritizing risk management, and greater executive board oversight. All of which results in a more cautious and less agile organization, and a culture that places greater scrutiny on the potential risks associated with new ventures, investments in R&D, mergers and acquisitions. After a period of risk stabilization following a corporate crisis, organizations don't typically remain permanently in an *'ultra-risk-averse'* state; and yet, the case studies presented in Chapter 5 indicate that the trauma of each crisis has lingered.

Phase 2: Execute the Corporate Trauma Playbook

Rationale: An organization suffering from Corporate Trauma is unable to effectively respond to the classic turnaround playbook. Serial failed turnaround attempts have cut costs, stabilized cash flow, and divested non-core or underperforming business units which has effectively left the organization on 'life support' . . . and with a faint pulse. In response to the two questions raised in Chapter 5 – concerning the potential for a new CEO to improve company performance and the likely success of adopting a classic turnaround playbook – from a Corporate Trauma perspective, the answers are 'no' and 'no'.

Assumptions: The principle behind the expression 'you can't cut your way to growth' captures the essence of failed serial turnaround attempts, where the defensive actions of cost-cutting and divestment of non-core business activities means that, after many years, there may not be much more to cut or sell. Endless cost reductions can stifle innovation, damage product or service quality, demotivate employees, and ultimately limit an organization's potential to innovate and grow. As such, the Corporate Trauma Playbook assumes that 'managing costs' and pursuing 'operational efficiencies' remain in play but should not be the primary drivers as they do not provide a route to strategic renewal, growth and overcoming a deep-seated trauma.

Secondly, as with all turnaround efforts, a robust performance measurement system needs to identify, track and report on relevant key performance indicators (KPIs) in order to drive change, performance and accountability. As noted above in Phase 1, these metrics will be company and industry specific. Therefore, strategically choose and regularly review relevant KPIs to monitor the organization's vital health signs.

The Corporate Trauma Playbook, visually outlined in Diagram 13 below, offers a structured approach to navigating and rectifying the long-term consequences of a significant corporate crisis. The centerpiece of the playbook focuses on the strategic renewal of an organization and once the strategic process of re-evaluating the vision, mission and core purpose has been completed, the other elements of the playbook should be activated. To gain immediate traction, this will not be a sequential rollout and different teams should begin implementing the tactical actions concurrently. This parallel approach to implementation is crucial for building momentum and belief in a new future. Remember that strategic renewal is an ongoing effort and each element of the playbook will be implemented with iterative cycles that continuously refine the approach.

Each element within this framework will now be explored in detail, accompanied by a clear rationale and a series of actionable tactics. While the suggested actions are not intended to be an exhaustive list, they highlight key considerations and practical steps that organizations can take to overcome trauma induced chronic underperformance. This playbook serves as a foundational guide and encourages readers to adapt the tactical actions to the unique circumstances of an organization suffering from Corporate Trauma.

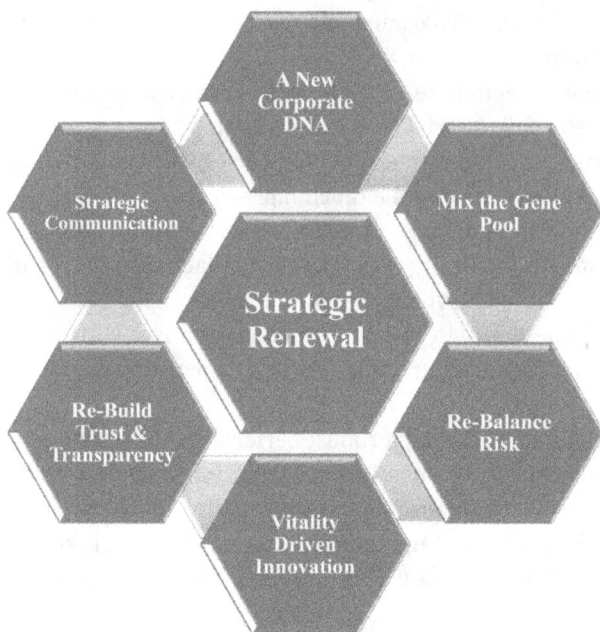

Diagram 13: The Corporate Trauma Playbook.

Strategic Renewal

Rationale: Strategic Renewal is about fundamentally rethinking an organization's purpose, direction and even the business model to position it for future growth, improved health and to ensure its long-term relevance and competitiveness. It is the centerpiece of the playbook with all the other elements supporting the aim to strategically renew, revitalize and grow an organization.

Strategic renewal focuses on a re-evaluation of the core purpose of the organization and the reason for its existence. This appraisal should renew the purpose and consider what new goals and aspirations should guide the organization, and examine how 'value' is created, delivered, and captured. This will mean exploring new revenue streams, optimizing cost structures, embracing digital transformation, or even completely pivoting to a different way of operating. This evaluation process should also anticipate future trends and identify new opportunities for growth by proactively considering new markets and developing innovative products or services. Strategic renewal addresses internal capabilities, culture, and rebuilding trust with stakeholders. A healthy organization is one that can adapt quickly, foster innovation, and attract and retain top talent to help maintain a crucial competitive edge.

Actionable Tactics

Conduct an External Strategic Analysis of the Evolving Environment and Identify Emerging Market Opportunities: The trauma and chronic underperformance of an organization underpins the need to fundamentally re-evaluate why the company exists and what it aspires to achieve. Undertake a deep-dive into the current and future market landscape by analyzing evolving customer needs, emerging competitive threats, disruptive technologies, changing regulatory frameworks, and broader macroeconomic trends. This analysis should help to identify new market segments, unmet customer needs, and potential opportunities for innovation, growth and differentiation.

Conduct an Internal Strategic Analysis of Core Competencies, Underutilized Assets, and Critical Resource Gaps: Conduct an assessment of the organization's existing strengths and capabilities by identifying core competencies that can be leveraged in new ways for existing and future markets. Furthermore, identify any underutilized assets or resources that could be redeployed and assess whether or not there are any significant resource gaps (skills, technology, infrastructure) that need to be addressed through investment, partnerships, or acquisitions.

Explore New Strategic Directions, Innovative Business Models, and Diversification Opportunities: In fundamentally rethinking an organization's purpose and direction, there needs to be a candid discussion about how the organization can be positioned for future growth. Be open to considering significant shifts in strategic direction, the business model and diversification into adjacent or new markets. Be brave and remember . . . the choice is clear: either boldly reset and revitalize the organization or endure the ongoing consequences of Corporate Trauma.

Reassess the Vision and Mission to Define a New Purpose: The strategic analysis above is an important step in helping to define a compelling new vision and mission. This analysis will provide the essential foundation for making informed decisions about the purpose and direction of the organization and how it can compete in a way that delivers value to customers and an edge over the competition. So, revisit your mission statement to ensure it still resonates with the current market environment and future competitive dynamics and create a compelling vision, informed by market realities and future opportunities, that will resonate with stakeholders. The new vision and mission should be supported with a strategy that clearly aims for growth, by competing in specific markets where value creation opportunities can deliver a sustainable competitive advantage.

A New Corporate DNA

Rationale: An organization with Corporate Trauma will have developed a culture of blame, risk aversion, and internal competition as employees try to protect their positions, authority and personal domains. These embedded defensive behaviors are a hidden killer of corporate vitality and act as significant barriers to the openness, collaboration, and the levels of innovative thinking that are needed for a successful turnaround and cultural shift.

Having 'reset' the organization with a fundamental rethinking of its purpose and direction to improve its health and secure future growth, it's time to get to work on developing a new cultural identity . . . a new corporate DNA!

It's likely to be a relatively long and arduous task that will require strong and consistent top-down leadership to change the often-deep-seated cynicism and low morale of employees who may not only have lived through the crisis that triggered the decline, but also have witnessed numerous failed turnaround attempts and changes in executive leadership. Leaders must be prepared for resistance and setbacks and maintain an unwavering commitment to cultural change; the alternative is to give up and return to a 'path dependent' culture of chronic underperformance.

The Corporate Trauma Playbook focuses on a fundamental shift, not just a superficial rebranding of the corporate culture. Injecting *'vitality'* into the new corporate DNA should focus on developing a culture of experimentation where a 'test and learn' and 'fail fast' provides an opportunity to learn, improve, adapt and pivot to new approaches and successful solutions to problems. Developing a new corporate DNA will require a multi-faceted and well-resourced approach that will include the following actions.

Define and Embed Core Values and Behaviors: Beyond simply stating new values, the process must involve a collaborative effort to define what these values truly mean in the context of daily work. Workshops, surveys, and focus groups can engage employees in articulating the specific behaviors that exemplify each value. For instance, if 'collaboration' is a new value, define what collaborative behaviors look like in meetings, project teams, and cross-departmental interactions. These defined behaviors should then be integrated into performance evaluations, training programs, and even informal recognition systems. Storytelling and sharing examples of employees embodying these values can further solidify their understanding and widespread adoption.

Lead by Example and Foster Cultural Champions: Leadership's role extends beyond mere endorsement of new cultural values and behaviors. Leaders at all levels must actively and visibly demonstrate the new cultural values in their decision-making, communication, and interactions. This requires ongoing coaching and development for leaders to ensure they are equipped to champion the desired culture. Identifying and empowering 'cultural champions' within the employee base – individuals who naturally embody the new values – can also be a powerful way to spread and reinforce the desired attitudes and behaviors. These champions can also act as informal mentors and role models.

Comprehensive Communication and Active Engagement: Communication about the cultural shift must be frequent, multi-faceted, and transparent. Beyond formal announcements, utilize storytelling, internal blogs, videos, and interactive platforms to illustrate the *'why'* behind the changes and the positive impact the new culture is expected to have. Crucially, actively solicit employee feedback through surveys, town hall Q&A sessions, and dedicated feedback channels. Demonstrate that employee input is valued and acted upon to foster a sense of ownership and co-creation.

Robust Reinforcement and Meaningful Recognition Systems: Integrate the new cultural values into formal performance management processes, ensuring that attitudes and behaviors are aligned with these values, and both recognized and rewarded accordingly. This could involve incorporating 'cultural fit' into performance reviews, creating specific awards for embodying core values, and publicly acknowledging individuals and teams that consistently demonstrate the desired behaviors. Ensure that recognition is timely, specific, and meaningful to the recipients.

Build Belief and Momentum with Quick Wins: Developing a new cultural DNA requires the active participation and buy-in of employees at all levels. In a struggling organization, apathy and disengagement can be significant hurdles, so celebrating early successes can generate excitement, build momentum and provide employees with examples of how the organization's new purpose, direction and cultural values are producing positive and tangible results. For example, a small, cross-functional team achieving a rapid improvement through better collaboration can demonstrate the value of teamwork and break down siloed thinking. Celebrating quick wins can generate a sense of progress which creates a positive feedback loop where early success can build confidence to engage with larger cultural change initiatives.

Strategic Onboarding and Continuous Cultural Integration: The onboarding process for new hires is a critical opportunity to introduce and embed the new corporate DNA from day one. Dedicated sessions on company values, expectations, and cultural norms should be a standard part of the onboarding program. Furthermore, cultural integration should be an ongoing process, reinforced through regular training, team-building activities, and internal communication campaigns that continuously highlight and celebrate the desired cultural attributes.

Mix the Gene Pool

Rationale: Organizations with a history of chronic underperformance and failed turnaround attempts will have undergone a series of severe cost cutting measures, widespread workforce reductions, and an exodus of top talent who sought more stable and promising environments. What's left behind . . . staff carrying the trauma of a historic crisis . . . staff who are dis-enfranchised and de-motivated . . . staff with low morale . . . staff with lowered expectations regarding the organization's future prospects . . . staff who are not engaged and less productive. It's an ideal environment for those employees with a tendency to embrace negativity, resist change, and complain about colleagues and new organizational initiatives. The terms 'deadwood', 'awkward squad' and 'axe grinders' are often used to describe these employees and cultivating a new corporate DNA will be difficult whilst they remain in the organization.

Mixing the gene pool by strategically hiring externally can be a powerful lever for cultural change in a chronically underperforming organization. The case studies in Chapter 5 demonstrated the practice of appointing internal candidates to the top job. Often regarded as a 'safe pair of hands' and with decades of company experience, these senior executives tend to operate within path-dependent culture, which makes it difficult for both them and the organization to change. Just as introducing individuals from a different population brings new genes into a gene pool, hiring externally brings in individuals with different backgrounds, experiences, perspectives, and importantly, 'dilutes' the existing dominant genes and enables new norms to emerge. Mixing the gene pool requires careful planning and execution to achieve a new cultural identity to ensure that the new corporate DNA takes root and leads to improved performance. It's not just about replacing existing employees; it's about thoughtfully introducing new perspectives and actively cultivating a new organizational identity.

Actionable Tactics

Identify Critical Skill Gaps Aligned with the New Strategic Direction and Targeted Recruitment: Before considering the widespread replacement of existing staff, conduct a thorough analysis of the skills and competencies required to execute the new strategic direction. Focus recruitment efforts specifically on filling critical skills gaps that cannot be addressed through internal training and development.

Implement Rigorous Performance Management Processes and Provide Opportunities for Improvement: Address individual performance issues by setting clear expectations, with regular feedback, improvement plans, and documented evaluations. Existing employees with low performance outcomes, a resistance to engage in re-training and those with a hostile attitude to change need to be replaced. No question!

Conduct a Thorough Cost-Benefit Analysis of Staff Replacement Versus Upskilling and Reskilling Initiatives: Carefully weigh the costs associated with recruitment, onboarding, severance, and potential productivity losses against the costs and benefits of investing in upskilling and reskilling existing employees. Remember that these costs are also an investment in a brighter future, where a new purpose, direction and culture will aim to improve the health of the organization and position it for long-term competitiveness and success.

Develop an Offboarding Plan for Transitions and New Onboarding: If existing employee replacement is deemed necessary, implement a well-communicated and supportive offboarding plan. This includes providing departing employees with fair severance packages and outplacement services. For new hires, develop a robust onboarding program that integrates them effectively into the new corporate culture and provides them with the necessary skills and knowledge.

Prioritize Effective Knowledge Transfer from Departing Employees to Minimize Operational Disruption: Before employees depart, implement structured processes for knowledge transfer, including documentation, training sessions, and mentorship opportunities. This is crucial to minimize disruption to ongoing operations and preserve valuable institutional knowledge.

Actively Pursue Strategic Partnerships, Collaborative Alliances, and Acquisitions: Engaging in a range of opportunities with external partners will provide access to new markets, technologies, talent, and distribution channels. However, it will also provide an opportunity to mix the gene pool between employees from different organizations and weaken the underperforming cultural norms that have contributed to previous failed turnaround attempts.

Re-Balance Risk

Rationale : In the wake of a significant corporate crisis, many organizations will be cautious and risk averse. This psychological outcome is both understandable and even necessary, but sustained periods of risk aversion lead to an enduring and dysfunctional adaption that suppresses innovation, hinders growth, and ultimately leads to stagnation. We have seen this consequence in the case studies presented in Chapter 5. This element of the playbook aims to move an organization from trauma to calculated growth by re-balancing attitudes to risk. It doesn't mean a return to the reckless practices that may have contributed to the initial crisis, however, it does aim to gradually shift the organizational mindset from fear of failure to a proactive pursuit of well-informed opportunities. It's about cultivating a culture of calculated risk-taking as part of the new corporate DNA, where opportunities are rigorously assessed, potential downsides are understood and mitigated, and strategic bets are made to drive sustainable growth and value creation.

Actionable Tactics

Take a Deep Dive into Risk Assessment: To gain a granular understanding of the current risk landscape and the depth of risk aversion, undertake an evaluation of the organization's strategy, governance policies and the processes and procedures that guide investment and spending decisions to identify biases towards risk avoidance. Follow this up with anonymous employee surveys and interviews across all levels to explore the underlying psychological and behavioral factors influencing risk decisions, and map risk aversion across different departments and business units to identify inconsistencies. Importantly, make a comparison of risk appetite from 'before and after' the date of the crisis that triggered the trauma. If necessary, engage external organizational psychologists or cultural change experts to undertake this work and to provide an objective perspective.

Executive Leadership Alignment Towards Calculated Risk-taking: The assessment of risk appetite in an organization will highlight that risk aversion is pervasive. Executive leaders now need to strike a balance between the caution learned from the crisis and the need to embrace innovation for future growth, competitiveness and the strategic renewal of the organization. So, conduct workshops with the executive team to discuss the impact of excessive risk aversion on long-term growth and develop a clear and compelling narrative about the 'new' approach to risk – emphasizing calculated risk, learning from the past, and embracing innovation for future success.

Enhance the Risk Management Framework: To ensure that the risk management infrastructure supports calculated risk-taking, rather than simply preventing all exposure to risk, refine policies and processes to better evaluate opportunities and potential rewards alongside potential downsides. Follow this with the training and development of staff to enhance risk literacy across the organization, focusing on risk-reward analysis. Piloting small scale innovation initiatives, with defined risk parameters, can be incorporated into the training program. This will create a controlled environment for experimenting with new ideas and gradually re-introduce a culture of innovation and measured risk-taking. The key to enhancing the risk management framework is to focus on evolution, not revolution!

Build Momentum with Safe-to-Fail Initiatives: Build momentum in the new approach to risk-taking by identifying specific areas with potential for innovation that align with the organization's strategic goals. Establish small, cross-functional teams with clear mandates and defined risk parameters for pilot projects to encourage experimentation. Creating projects where failure has limited negative consequences will build confidence and momentum; it will also provide valuable opportunities to learn from both successes and failures following the introduction of a more balanced approach to risk and innovation. Follow this up by recognizing and rewarding individuals and teams that have demonstrated a balanced approach to risk to achieve growth targets.

Vitality Driven Innovation

Rationale: The case studies presented in Chapter 5 illustrate that these companies have demonstrated that innovative thinking and activity has suffered as a result of a Corporate Trauma that has manifested as increased risk aversion, decreased investment in innovation (even if not explicitly reported), and an ongoing cycle of turnaround attempts that haven't fully reignited sustainable growth. To break free from this cycle, an organization suffering from a long-term decline in innovation needs to embrace a proactive and energized pursuit of new opportunities.

However, simply making significant investments in R&D (e.g. BlackBerry) will not guarantee a return on investment. Vitality Driven Innovation focuses on enabling and supporting innovation-led growth by generating revenue from activities that lead to new products or services. It's about injecting *'vitality'* into the new corporate DNA in order to stimulate long-term growth. So, the new vision and mission should create a compelling picture of the future, informed by market realities and opportunities, that will resonate with stakeholders, including employees, customers, and investors. It should also be supported with a strategic approach that aims for growth, by competing in specific markets where value creation opportunities can deliver a sustainable competitive advantage. As such, the following activities will foster a culture of 'vitality driven innovation' that will create new sources of value in chosen markets.

Actionable Tactics

Cultivate a Culture of Continuous Improvement, Experimentation, and Learning: A new corporate DNA should create an organizational culture that actively encourages curiosity, rewards experimentation (even failures that yield learning), and empowers employees at all levels to contribute new ideas. Implement mechanisms for capturing and sharing ideas, such as suggestion boxes, innovation platforms, and cross-functional brainstorming sessions. Regularly review processes and performance to identify ongoing opportunities for efficiency gains.

Empower Employee Involvement, Soliciting Improvement Ideas, and Invest in Training: Recognize that employees often have the best understanding of day-to-day operational challenges. Actively seek out employee input for improvements through suggestion programs, hands-on workshops, and collaborative problem-solving efforts within teams. Furthermore, invest in training and development to give employees the skills and knowledge they need to work more efficiently and contribute to optimizing processes.

Strategically Invest in Research and Development, Allocating Resources for Future Growth, and Exploring Emerging Technologies: Dedicate a portion of resources to research and development activities that explore new technologies, products, services, and business models. Stay abreast of emerging technologies and assess their potential application within the organization to ensure that any innovation investments are aligned with the overall strategic direction.

Actively Embrace Open Innovation, Collaborating with External Partners, and Leveraging External Expertise: Innovation doesn't always have to be an internal process. Organizations should actively look externally for fresh ideas, cutting-edge technologies, and diverse perspectives. This means seeking out collaborations with external partners like universities, start-ups, specialized research institutions, and even customers. Engaging in industry consortia and exploring strategic alliances are also excellent ways to cultivate a richer environment for innovation.

Establish Clear Processes for Idea Generation, Rigorous Evaluation, and Efficient Development: Implement a structured process for managing the innovation lifecycle, from initial idea generation through evaluation, prototyping, testing, and eventual implementation. Establish clear criteria for evaluating the potential of new ideas and allocate resources effectively to promising initiatives.

Invest in Innovation Hubs and Innovation Champions: Introduce innovation hubs, either physical or virtual, to foster innovation, entrepreneurship, and the exchange of ideas among various stakeholders. The hubs should be led by people who exhibit an entrepreneurial spirit and a passion for innovation with the aim of stimulating creativity, developing new ideas, processes, products or services that can drive growth.

Encourage Rapid Experimentation, Agile Prototyping, and Iterative Development: Foster a mindset of rapid experimentation and agile development by creating small-scale pilot projects to test new ideas and market acceptance with limited initial risk exposure. This process will require the need to embrace iterative development and incorporating feedback from testing and early adopters to refine and improve innovations.

Create a Safe Environment for Learning from Failure, Embracing Risk-Taking, and Celebrating Innovation Successes: Cultivate a culture where failure is viewed as a valuable learning opportunity, not a cause for blame. Encourage calculated risk-taking with 'safe-to-fail' pilot programs in the pursuit of developing a vitality driven innovation culture and publicly recognize and celebrate innovation successes to reinforce the importance of creative thinking and experimentation.

Develop a Robust Intellectual Property Strategy, Protecting Innovations, and Leveraging IP Assets: Establishing a robust intellectual property (IP) strategy is crucial for developing and protecting a vitality driven innovation strategy to support the strategic renewal of an organization. It's not enough to simply have innovative ideas; they must be actively protected. This means meticulously planning how to safeguard the organization's valuable creations through a combination of patents, trademarks, copyrights, and trade secrets. Beyond mere protection, actively manage and leverage these IP assets to forge competitive advantages to generate vitality driven revenue.

Introduce a New Product Vitality Index (NPVI): This metric measures the revenue generated from new products or services as a percentage of total revenue. The purpose of the index is to guide organizations in adopting more progressive and effective management practices by assessing their innovation output and ability to generate revenue growth through new offerings. A higher NPVI is generally correlated with a more innovative and dynamic organizations and its measurement can not only drive the development of innovative new products and services, but also new revenue streams.

Re-Build Trust and Transparency

Rationale: Rebuilding trust and transparency with stakeholders after a corporate crisis, particularly after a fraudulent wrongdoing, is not just a matter of ethical obligation, but a crucial strategic imperative for the long-term survival and success of an organization. The case studies in Chapter 5 identified that investors had abandoned each company as demonstrated by a significant and long-term decline in market capitalization. Benchmarked against 'best-in-class' companies, the extent of each firm's Corporate Trauma and lack of investor confidence was laid bare. Re-building brand reputation with demonstrable efforts to rectify past missteps can be a slow process of restoring the brand image with stakeholders, however, restoring trust will open doors to potential new investors and may even entice some previous shareholders to return which will improve market valuation.

It's a long and challenging process, but one that is absolutely necessary for recovery and strategic renewal. The following activities will help restore legitimacy, attract investment, retain customers and talented employees, strengthen stakeholder relationships, and ultimately ensure the long-term sustainability and ethical operation of the organization.

Actionable Tactics

Sincere Acknowledgement, Full Accountability, and Meaningful Apologies: The crisis that triggered the long-term chronic underperformance and trauma occurred years ago. So, re-look at company statements and apologies to assess whether the public acknowledgement of the specific failures and missteps that led to the crisis were sufficient. This includes being transparent about the 'root causes' identified through the internal investigation during Phase 1: Trauma Assessment and Diagnosis. If the public apologies were sincere, genuine, empathetic and clearly articulated the organization's remorse for the impact on stakeholders, then great . . . it's time to move on. If not, apologize with sincerity once more, and communicate that a new chapter in the organization's history has begun with a clear and compelling new vision and mission that will inspire stakeholders.

Demonstrate Concrete Actions and Tangible Improvements: Words alone are insufficient to rebuild trust. Stakeholders need to see tangible evidence of change in the form of stronger corporate governance structures, internal controls, and ethical guidelines, making the organization more resilient to future crises. This evidence of change also includes demonstrating 'how' implementing the new vision, mission and strategy has renewed and re-vitalized the organization in a way that has delivered value to customers and revenues from new products or services. Importantly, regularly communicate how this strategic renewal has been achieved by adhering to ethical practices and a genuine commitment to addressing the issues that caused the crisis.

Active Listening, Empathizing, and Incorporating Stakeholder Feedback: Create formal mechanisms for gathering stakeholder feedback, such as surveys, advisory boards, and regular consultations. Demonstrate that this feedback is not just collected but actively considered and incorporated into decision-making processes.

Ensure Transparency in Decision-Making Processes (Where Appropriate and Feasible): While not all internal deliberations can be public, strive for transparency in the rationale behind key decisions, particularly those directly impacting stakeholders. Explain the factors considered, the trade-offs made, and how stakeholder interests were taken into account. This fosters a sense of fairness and understanding. A commitment to transparency will also help to regain the trust of regulatory bodies which is crucial for potentially mitigating future scrutiny or penalties.

Maintain Consistent Actions and Build a Track Record of Reliability: Consistency is paramount. Ensure that the organization's actions constantly align with its stated commitments and values. Over time, building a track record of reliability and integrity will be crucial in restoring stakeholder confidence. Furthermore, recognize that any deviation from stated principles will severely undermine trust levels.

Focus on Mutual Value Creation and Long-Term Relationships: Demonstrate a renewed commitment to creating mutual value for all stakeholders. For customers, this means delivering superior products and services; for investors, sustainable profitability and growth; for employees, a fair and supportive work environment; and for the community, responsible corporate citizenship. Focus on building long-term, mutually beneficial relationships based on trust and shared goals as an improved reputation can become a significant differentiator and a source of long-term competitive advantage.

Strategic Communication

Rationale: The importance of strategic communication to the Corporate Trauma Playbook cannot be underestimated. Simply put, there is a lot to communicate about the strategic renewal of the organization (e.g. a new vision, mission, purpose) and this element of the playbook needs to be pre-planned, sufficiently resourced and conveyed to all stakeholders (particularly investors) at the earliest opportunity. The strategic communication plan needs to ensure that the messaging is consistent across all functions and platforms and that everyone within the organization is working towards the same communication objectives to advance the new vision, mission and strategic goals. In essence, this part of the playbook aims to develop a clear and compelling narrative that will resonate with all stakeholders about the organization's new strategic direction and a vitality driven innovation strategy that will focus on specific markets where value creation can lead to a sustainable competitive advantage.

Actionable Tactics

Craft a Compelling, Truthful, and Adaptive Narrative: The narrative should clearly articulate the lessons learned from the crisis that triggered the long-term underperformance and trauma of the organization. It must be grounded in truth and authenticity, acknowledging both historic and current underperformance, while painting a credible picture of future success. This narrative should be adaptable, evolving as the turnaround progresses and new milestones are achieved.

Establish Open, Consistent, and Multi-Directional Communication Channels: Employ a diverse range of communication channels to reach different audiences effectively. This includes formal channels like press releases, annual reports, and investor calls, as well as informal channels like social media, internal blogs, and employee forums. Ensure that messaging is consistent across all channels while being adapted to the specific medium, and that the timing and cadence of communications should aim to maximize impact and actively solicit and respond to stakeholder inquiries and concerns.

Understand Key Audiences and Precisely Tailor Messages: Go beyond broad communication. Develop a nuanced understanding of the specific concerns, information needs, and communication preferences of each key stakeholder group. Tailor messages to resonate with each audience, addressing their specific anxieties and highlighting the information most relevant to them. For example, investors will be interested in financial performance and strategic milestones, while employees will focus on job security and the new company culture.

Proactive, Transparent, and Empathetic Communication: Proactively communicate key developments, progress updates, and even potential challenges faced by the strategic renewal of the organization. When facing difficulties, communicate with empathy, acknowledging the concerns of stakeholders.

Actively Monitor and Analyze Sentiment in Real-Time: Implement robust monitoring systems to track media coverage, social media sentiment, and stakeholder feedback. Analyze this information to understand how the strategic renewal of the organization is being received and identify any emerging concerns or misunderstandings. Be prepared to adapt communication strategies and messaging in real-time based on this feedback. Importantly, analyze the sentiment of internal and external communications for the content and emotional tone in order to assess whether the outputs support the organization's new strategic direction. As we have seen in the case studies in Chapter 5, the analysis of annual reports for innovation and risk words found a *'hidden trauma'* for each company in terms of being more risk averse following a crisis.

Ensure a Seamless Alignment Between Internal and External Communications: Internal communications must be aligned with external messaging to ensure consistency and build trust among employees. Equip employees with the information and talking points they need to effectively communicate the organization's narrative to external parties.

Develop a Robust and Agile Crisis Communication Preparedness Plan: The previous corporate crisis should have provided an important opportunity to learn about what worked, or didn't work in the former crisis management plan. A new or updated plan should provide a comprehensive, pre-emptive strategy designed to guide an organization's actions and communications before, during, and after a significant crisis event.

Appendices

Appendix 1: Innovation and Risk words used to assess Cultural Adaptation

Low Innovation	Medium Innovation	High Innovation
addition	advance	bet
alteration	contemporary	creativity
development	change	cutting edge
enhance	departure	ingenuity
existing	deviation	imagination
evolve	evolution	inspiration
improvement	expand	inventive
launch	forward-looking	leading edge
modify	growth	novelty
proceed	increase	originality
product development	improvement	revolution
progress	introduction	shift
research	innovate	transformation
upgrade	modern	unique
variation	new	vision

Low Risk	Medium Risk	High Risk
cessation	assumption	chance
closure	contingency	destiny
consequence	difficulty	fortune
concern	doubt	gamble
damage	exposure	guess
danger	liable	imagine
end	likelihood	luck
hazard	option	openness
jeopardy	possibility	opportunity
loss	probability	outlook
peril	prospect	possibility
plunge	protect	prospect
termination	risk	shot in the dark
threat	trouble	speculate
vulnerable	uncertainty	venture

https://doi.org/10.1515/9783111571126-007

Appendix 2: Corporate Trauma: case study matrix

Company	Crisis Year	No. CEOs	Adverse CEO Tenure[1]	Adverse Share Price Adaptation[2]	Adverse Financial Adaptation	Adverse Cultural Adaptation
AIG	2005	7	✓	✓	✓	✓
Barclays	2012	5	✓	✓	✓	✓
BlackBerry	2011	5	✓	✓	✓	✓
BP	2010	3	✓	✓	✓	✓
Wells Fargo	2016	3	✓	✓	✓	✓
VW	2015	3	✓	✓	✗	✓

Footnotes
1. Benchmarked against the 9.3 years of S&P 500 companies during 2020.
2. Benchmarked against the S&P 1200 Global Index

Notes

Chapter 2: A Brief History Of Epigenetics

1. Steves CJ, Spector TD, Jackson SH. Ageing, genes, environment and epigenetics: what twin studies tell us now, and in the future. Age Ageing. 2012 Sept;41(5):581–6.
2. Bell JT, Spector TD. A twin approach to unraveling epigenetics. Trends in Genetics. 2011 Mar;27 (3):116–25.
3. van Dongen J, Gordon SD, McRae AF, Odintsova VV, Mbarek H, Breeze CE, et al. Identical twins carry a persistent epigenetic signature of early genome programming. Nature Communications. 2021 Sep; 23;12(1):5618.
4. Kaati G, Bygren LO, Pembrey M, Sjostrom M. Transgenerational response to nutrition, early life circumstances and longevity. European Journal of Human Genetics. 2007 Jul;15(7):784.
5. Davidson AC, Mellor DJ. The adjustment of children of Australian Vietnam veterans: is there evidence for the transgenerational transmission of the effects of war-related trauma? Australian and New Zealand Journal of Psychiatry. 2001 Jun;35(3):345–51.
6. Neigh GN, Ritschel LA, Nemeroff CB. Biological consequences and transgenerational impact of violence and abuse. Psychiatric Times. 2010 Nov;27(11):49–52.
7. Yehuda R, Daskalakis NP, Lehrner A, Desarnaud F, Bader HN, Makotkine I, et al. Influences of maternal and paternal PTSD on epigenetic regulation of the glucocorticoid receptor gene on Holocaust survivor offspring. American Journal of Psychiatry. 2016 Sep;173(9):872–80.
8. Sarigedik E, Naldemir IF, Karaman AK, Altinsoy HB. Intergenerational transmission of psychological trauma: A structural neuroimaging study. Psychiatry Research: Neuroimaging. 2022 Sep 30;326:111538.
9. Yehuda R, Engel SM, Brand SR, Seckl J, Marcus SM, Berkowitz GS. Transgenerational effects of post-traumatic stress disorder in babies of mothers exposed to the World Trade Center attacks during pregnancy. The Journal of Clinical Endocrinology & Metabolism. 2005 Jul;90(7):4115–8.
10. Berkowitz GS, Wolff MS, Janevic TM, Holzman IR, Yehuda R, Landrigan PJ. The World Trade Center disaster and intrauterine growth restriction. The Journal of the American Medical Association. 2003 Aug 6;290(5):595–6.
11. Marchese S, Cancelmo L, Diab O, Cahn L, Aaronson C, Daskalakis NP, et al. Altered gene expression and PTSD symptom dimensions in World Trade Center responders. Molecular Psychiatry. 2022 Apr;27(4):2225–46.
12. Tuscher JJ, Day JJ. Multigenerational epigenetic inheritance: One step forward, two generations back. Neurobiology of Disease. 2019 Dec;132:104591.
13. Darnaudéry M, Maccari S. Epigenetic programming of the stress response in male and female rats by prenatal restraint stress. Brain Research Reviews. 2008 Apr;57(2):571–85.
14. Serpeloni F, Radtke K, de Assis SG, Henning F, Nätt D, Elbert T. Grandmaternal stress during pregnancy and DNA methylation of the third generation: an epigenome-wide association study. Translational Psychiatry. 2017 Aug 15;7(8):e1202.
15. Scharf M. Long-term effects of trauma: Psychosocial functioning of the second and third generation of Holocaust survivors. Development and Psychopathology. 2007 Spring;19 (2):603–22.

https://doi.org/10.1515/9783111571126-008

16. Danieli Y, Norris FH, Engdahl B. A question of who, not if: Psychological disorders in Holocaust survivors' children. Psychological Trauma: Theory, research, practice, and policy,. 2017 Feb;9 (Suppl 1):98–106.

17. DeAngelis T. The legacy of trauma: An emerging line of research is exploring how historical and cultural traumas affect survivors' children for generations to come. Monitor on Psychology. 2019 Feb;50(2).

18. Rothstein MA, Cai Y, Marchant GE. The ghost in our genes: legal and ethical implications of epigenetics. Health Matrix. 2009 Winter;19(1):1–62.

Chapter 3: Diagnosing Corporate Trauma

1. Edvardsson B, Roos I. Critical incident techniques: towards a framework for analysing the criticality of critical incidents. International Journal of Service Industry Management. 2001;12 (3):251–68.

2. Bott G, Tourish D. The critical incident technique reappraised: using critical incidents to illuminate organizational practices and build theory. Qualitative Research in Organizations and Management: An International Journal. 2016;11(4):276–300.

3. Fagiano D. Altering the corporate DNA. Management Review. 1994;83(12):4.

4. Dyer JH, Gregersen HB, Christensen CM. The innovator's DNA. Harvard Business Review. 2009;87(12):60–7.

5. Meyerson B. Embedding innovation in corporate DNA. Research-Technology Management. 2016;59(6):30–5.

6. Chen Y, Ibhagui OW. R&D-firm performance nexus: new evidence from NASDAQ listed firms. The North American Journal of Economics and Finance. 2019;50:101009.

7. Yeh M-L, Chu H-P, Sher PJ, Chiu Y-C. R&D intensity, firm performance and the identification of the threshold: fresh evidence from the panel threshold regression model. Applied Economics. 2010;42(3):389–401.

8. Oliver JJ. Strategic transformations in the media. Journal of Media Business Studies. 2018;15 (4):278–99.

9. You Y, Srinivasan S, Pauwels K, Joshi A. How CEO/CMO characteristics affect innovation and stock returns: findings and future directions. Journal of the Academy of Marketing Science. 2020;48:1229–53.

10. Stohl C, Stohl M, Popova L. A new generation of corporate codes of ethics. Journal of Business Ethics. 2009;90:607–22.

11. Cates SV. Generational management in corporate America: the differences and challenges in management of four generations of working adults. Chinese Business Review. 2010;9 (8):46–54.

12. Tonello M, Schloetzer J, McKenna F. CEO Succession Practices in the Russell 3000 and S&P500, The Conference Board [Internet]. 2021 [Accessed 2024 October 25]. Available from: https://corpgov.law.harvard.edu

Chapter 4: Corporate PTSD: When Crises Leave Lasting Scars

1. Liu Y, Shankar V, Yun W. Crisis management strategies and the long-term effects of product recalls on firm value. Journal of Marketing. 2017;81(5):30–48.
2. Wei J, Ouyang Z, Chen H. Well known or well liked? The effects of corporate reputation on firm value at the onset of a corporate crisis. Strategic Management Journal. 2017;38(10):2103–20.
3. Yakut E, Bayraktaroglu AG. Consumer reactions to product recalls: the effects of intentionality, reputation, and public apology on purchase intentions. Journal of Business Economics. 2021;91 (4):527–64.
4. Barker VL, Duhaime IM. Strategic change in the turnaround process: Theory and empirical evidence. Strategic Management Journal. 1997;18:13–38.
5. Morrow JL, Johnson RA, Busenitz LW. The effects of cost and asset retrenchment on firm performance: The overlooked role of a firm's competitive environment. Journal of Management. 2004;30:271–83.
6. Mitroff II, Shrivastava P, Udwadia FE. Effective crisis management. Academy of Management Perspectives. 1987;1(4):283–92.
7. Gruber DA, Smerek RE, Thomas-Hunt MC, James EH. The real-time power of Twitter: Crisis management and leadership in an age of social media. Business Horizons. 2015;58(2):163–72.
8. Parise S, Guinan PJ, Kafka R. Solving the crisis of immediacy: How digital technology can transform the customer experience. Business Horizons. 2016;59(4):411–20.
9. Oliver JJ. Is "transgenerational response" a hidden cause of failed corporate turnarounds and chronic underperformance? Strategy & Leadership. 2017;45(3):23–9.
10. Gusfield JR. General Education as a Career: a sociological analysis. The Journal of General Education. 1957;10(1):37–48.
11. Presthus RV. Behavior and bureaucracy in many cultures. Public Administration Review. 1959;25–35.
12. Schein EH. Defining organizational culture. Classics of Organization Theory. 1985;3(1):490–502.
13. Schneider B, Goldstiein HW, Smith DB. The ASA framework: An update. Personnel Psychology. 1995;48(4):747–73.
14. Epstein MJ, Buhovac AR, Yuthas K. Implementing sustainability: The role of leadership and organizational culture. Strategic Finance. 2010;91(10):41.
15. Groysberg B, Lee J, Price J, Cheng J. The leader's guide to corporate culture. Harvard Business Review. 2018;96(1):44–52.
16. Mintzberg H, Ahlstrand B, Lampel JB. Strategy safari: The complete guide through the wilds of strategic management. Pearson UK; 2020.
17. Fagiano D. Altering the corporate DNA. Management Review. 1994;83(12):4.
18. Dyer JH, Gregersen HB, Christensen CM. The innovator's DNA. Harvard Business Review. 2009;87(12):60–7.
19. Meyerson B. Embedding innovation in corporate DNA. Research-Technology Management. 2016;59(6):30–5.
20. Kiechel W. Lords of strategy: The secret intellectual history of the new corporate world. Harvard Business Press; 2010.
21. Oliver JJ. Corporate turnaround failure: is the proper diagnosis transgenerational response? Strategy & Leadership. 2020;48(3):1–7.
22. Lorsch JW. Managing culture: the invisible barrier to strategic change. California Management Review. 1986;28(2):95–109.

23. Mintzberg H, Ahlstrand B, Lampel J. Strategy Safari: A guided tour through the wilds of strategic management. FT Prentice Hall; 1998.

24. Groysberg B, Lee J, Price J, Cheng J. The leader's guide to corporate culture. Harvard Business Review. 2018;96(1):44–52.

25. Hurley RF, Hult GTM. Innovation, market orientation, and organizational learning: An integration and empirical examination. Journal of Marketing.1998;62(3):42–54.

26. Han JK, Kim N, Srivastava RK. Market orientation and organizational performance: Is innovation a missing link? Journal of Marketing. 1998;62(4):30–45.

27. Boston Consulting Group. Overcoming the Innovation Readiness Gap: Most Innovative Companies. 2023. [Accessed 8 November 2024]. Available from: https://www.bcg.com/publica tions/2023/advantages-through-innovation-in-uncertain-times

28. Denrell J. Organizational risk taking: Adaptation versus variable risk preferences. Industrial and Corporate Change. 2008;17(3):427–66.

29. Kung L. Strategic management in the media: from theory to practice. London: Sage; 2024.

30. Bowman EH. Risk seeking by troubled firms. Sloan Management Review. 1982;23(4):33.

31. Garvin DA. Building a learning organization. Harvard Business Review. 1993;71(4):73–91.

32. Fiegenbaum A, Thomas H. Attitudes toward risk and the risk–return paradox: Prospect theory explanations. Academy of Management Journal. 1988;31(1):85–106.

33. Das RC. Interplays among R&D spending, patent and income growth: new empirical evidence from the panel of countries and groups. Journal of Innovation and Entrepreneurship. 2020;9 (1):1–22.

34. Hirschey M, Skiba H, Wintoki MB. The size, concentration and evolution of corporate R&D spending in US firms from 1976 to 2010: Evidence and implications. Journal of Corporate Finance. 2012;18(3):496–518.

35. Guo B, Wang J, Wei SX. R&D spending, strategic position and firm performance. Frontiers of Business Research in China. 2018;12(1):1–19.

36. Barker III VL, Mueller GC. CEO characteristics and firm R&D spending. Management Science. 2002;48(6):782–801.

37. You Y, Srinivasan S, Pauwels K, Joshi A. How CEO/CMO characteristics affect innovation and stock returns: findings and future directions. Journal of the Academy of Marketing Science. 2020;48:1229–53.

38. Oliver JJ, Exploring the Influence of CEO Traits on Media Firm Innovation and Performance. International Journal on Media Management. 2025;1–22. Available from: https://doi.org/10. 1080/14241277.2025.2481872

39. Weisbach MS. Outside directors and CEO turnover. Journal of Financial Economics. 1988;20:431–60.

40. Brickley JA. Empirical research on CEO turnover and firm-performance: A discussion. Journal of Accounting and Economics. 2003;36(1–3):227–33.

41. Groysberg B, Lee J, Price J, Cheng J. The leader's guide to corporate culture. Harvard Business Review. 2018;96(1):44–52.

42. CEO and Executive Compensation Practices in the Russell 3000 and S&P 500. Harvard Law School Forum on Corporate Governance [Accessed 23 November]. Available from: https://corpgov.law.harvard.edu/lawfirm/the-conference-board/

43. Oliver JJ. Is "transgenerational response" a hidden cause of failed corporate turnarounds and chronic underperformance? Strategy & Leadership. 2017;45(3):23–9.

Chapter 5: Diagnosing Cases Of Corporate Trauma

1. Eisenhardt KM. Building theories from case study research. Academy of Management Review. 1989 Oct;14(4):532–50.
2. Yin RK. Case Study Research: Design and Methods. London, UK: Sage; 1994.
3. Gibbert M, Ruigrok W, Wicki B. What passes as a rigorous case study?. Strategic Management Journal. 2008 Dec;29(13):1465–74.
4. Oliver JJ. Scenario planning: Reflecting on cases of actionable knowledge. Futures & Foresight Science. 2023 Sep;5(3–4):e164.
5. Oliver JJ. Managing Media Firms: case studies of practice-led research, actionable knowledge, and instrumental impact. In: Media Management Matters. London: Taylor & Francis; 2020. p. 59–74.
6. Yehuda R, Engel SM, Brand SR, Seckl J, Marcus SM, Berkowitz GS. Transgenerational effects of post-traumatic stress disorder in babies of mothers exposed to the World Trade Center attacks during pregnancy. The Journal of Clinical Endocrinology & Metabolism. 2005 Jul;90(7):4115–8.
7. Berkowitz GS, Wolff MS, Janevic TM, Holzman IR, Yehuda R, Landrigan PJ. The World Trade Center disaster and intrauterine growth restriction. The Journal of the American Medical Association. 2003 Aug 6;290(5):595–6.

AIG: Doing what it does best. . .but fraudulently!

1. American International Group Inc. 2009 Annual Report. 2009:3.
2. AIG Program Status. U.S. Department of the Treasury [Internet]. [Accessed 2024 Dec 5]. Available from: https://home.treasury.gov/data/troubled-assets-relief-program/aig/status
3. U.S. Securities and Exchange Commission. Complaint against Defendants Maurice R. Greenberg and Howard I. Smith. August 6, 2009.
4. AIG Settles Fraud, Bid-rigging And Improper Accounting Charges. New York State Attorney General [Internet]. 2006 [Accessed 2024 Nov 29]. Available from: https://ag.ny.gov/press-release/2006/aig-settles-fraud-bid-rigging-and-improper-accounting-charges
5. Share Price Performance of AIG v S&P Global 1200 Index (2004–2025) [Internet]. [Accessed 2024 Dec 2]. Available from: https://www-capitaliqcom.bournemouth.idm.oclc.org
6. American International Group Inc. 2013 Annual Report. 2013:2–3.
7. American International Group Inc. 2012 Annual Report. 2012:2–10.
8. American International Group Inc. 2008 Annual Report. 2008:1.
9. American International Group Inc. 2014 Annual Report. 2014:1.
10. AIG CEO Peter Hancock to resign. Reuters [Internet]. 2017 Mar 9 [Accessed 2024 Dec 10]. Available from: https://www.reuters.com/article/markets/europe/aig-ceo-peter-hancock-to-resign-idUSASB0B4NK/
11. American International Group Inc. 2018 Annual Report. 2018:3.
12. Peter S. Zaffino Appointed President of AIG [Internet]. U.S. Securities and Exchange Commission. 2019 Aug 2 [Accessed 2024 Dec 10]. Available from: https://www.sec.gov/Archives/edgar/data/5272/000110465919073581/tm1926473d1_ex99-1.htm
13. American International Group Inc. 2023 Annual Report. 2023:3.
14. American International Group Inc. 2024 Annual Report. 2024:1–2.

Barclays: If you ain't cheating, you ain't trying

1. FCA fines Barclays £40 million. Financial Conduct Authority [Internet]. 2022 Dec 16 [Accessed 2025 Jan 7]. Available from: https://www.fca.org.uk/news/press-releases/fca-fines-barclays-40-million

2. Our Strategy explained. Barclays PLC [Internet]. [Accessed 2025 Jan 7]. Available from: https://home.barclays/who-we-are/our-strategy/

3. FINAL NOTICE. Financial Services Authority [Internet]. 2012 Jun 27 [Accessed 2025 Jan 7]. Available from: https://www.fca.org.uk/publication/final-notices/barclays-jun12.pdf

4. Barclays boss Bob Diamond resigns amid Libor scandal. BBC News [Internet]. 2012 Jul 3 [Accessed 2025 Jan 7]. Available from: https://www.bbc.co.uk/news/business

5. Share Price Performance of Barclays v S&P Global 1200 Index (2012–2025). Capital IQ [Internet]. [Accessed 2025 Jan 7]. Available from: https://www-capitaliqcom.bournemouth.idm.oclc.org.

6. Consent Order in the Matter of Barclays Bank, PLC. The New York State Department of Financial Services. 2015 May 19.

7. Never Again? Risk Management in Banking beyond the Credit Crisis. KPMG International; 2009.

8. Barclays lifts outlook as windfall from high interest rates endures. Financial Times [Internet]. 2023 Oct 26 [Accessed 2025 Jan 10]. Available from: https://www.ft.com/content/3cdf0ffa-b46e-459b-b11e-1ccd47c97f11

9. Barclays bank CEO Diamond resigns amid scandal. CNN [Internet]. 2012 Jul 3 [Accessed 2025 Jan 13]. Available from: https://edition.cnn.com/2012/07/03/business/barclays-diamond-resigns/index.html

10. Barclays PLC. 2012 Annual Report. p. 8.

11. Barclays sacks boss Antony Jenkins in row over strategy. BBC News [Internet]. 2015 Jul 8 [Accessed 2025 Jan 13]. Available from: https://www.bbc.co.uk/news/business-33438914

12. James E. Staley appointed as Group Chief Executive. Barclays PLC Press Release. 2015 Oct 28.

13. Barclays PLC. 2016 Annual Report. p. 4.

14. Barclays PLC. 2018 Annual Report. p. 5.

15. Decision Notice, Mr James Edward Staley. Financial Conduct Authority; 2023 May 30.

16. Barclays PLC. 2021 Annual Report. p. 7.

17. Barclays PLC. 2023 Annual Report. p. 8–9.

BlackBerry: Its life Jim, but not as we know it

1. Interbrand's Top 100 global brands 2009. Campaign Live [Internet]. 2009 [Accessed 2025 Jan 20]. Available from: https://www.campaignlive.co.uk/article/interbrands-top-100-global-brands-2009

2. Obama Digs In for His BlackBerry. New York Times [Internet]. 2009 Jan 8 [Accessed 2025 Jan 20]. Available from: https://www.nytimes.com/2009/01/08/us/politics/08berry.html#

3. Oliver JJ. Chronic corporate performance in Media-Tech firms: a new perspective. Journal of Media Business Studies. 2021;18(4):1–22.

4. BlackBerry. Investor Overview [Internet]. [Accessed 2025 Jan 20]. Available from: https://investors.blackberry.com/

5. RIM's long road to reinvent the BlackBerry. The Globe and Mail [Internet]. [Accessed 2025 Jan 21]. Available from: www.theglobeandmail.com/globe-investor/rims-long-road-to-reinvent-the-blackberry/article7901031/

6. RIM shares down on BlackBerry revenue miss. phys.org [Internet]. 2011 Mar [Accessed 2025 Jan 21]. Available from: https://phys.org/news/2011-03-maker-blackberry-pct.html

7. BlackBerry 10: Re-designed, Re-engineered, and Re-invented [Internet]. blackberry.com. 2013 [Accessed 2025 Jan 21]. Available from: www.blackberry.com/us/en/company/newsroom/press-releases/2013/blackberry-10-re-designed-re-engineered-and-re-invented

8. Share Price Performance of BlackBerry v S&P Global 1200 Index (2010–2025) [Internet]. Capital IQ. [Accessed 2025 Jan 21]. Available from: https://www-capitaliqcom.bournemouth.idm.oclc.org

9. Oliver J. Exploring the Influence of CEO Traits on Media Firm Innovation and Performance. International Journal on Media Management. 2025:1–22. Available from: https://doi.org/10.1080/14241277.2025.2481872

10. RIM's Balsillie, Lazaridis resign. CBC News [Internet]. 2012 Jan 22 [Accessed 2025 Jan 27]. Available from: https://www.cbc.ca/news/business/rim-s-balsillie-lazaridis-resign

11. Research In Motion Limited. 2012 Annual Report. 2012;15.

12. BlackBerry fires CEO Thorsten Heins as $4.7bn Fairfax rescue bid collapses. The Guardian [Internet]. 2013 Nov 4 [Accessed 2025 Jan 27]. Available from: https://www.theguardian.com/technology/2013/nov/04/blackberry-fires-ceo-thorsten-heins-fairfax-bid-collapses

13. New BlackBerry boss John Chen out to prove skeptics wrong. Reuters [Internet]. 2013 Nov 4 [Accessed 2025 Jan 28]. Available from: https://www.reuters.com/article/us-blackberry-offer-strategy-idUKBRE9A30PH20131104/

14. Research In Motion Limited. 2014 Annual Report. 2014;12.

15. BlackBerry Completes Acquisition of Cylance [Internet]. blackberry.com. 2019 Feb 21 [Accessed 2025 Jan 29]. Available from: https://www.blackberry.com/us/en/company/newsroom/press-releases/2019/blackberry-completes-acquisition-of-cylance

16. Letter to BlackBerry Employees from John Chen. BlackBerry News [Internet]. 2023 Oct 30 [Accessed 2025 Jan 29]. Available from: https://blogs.blackberry.com/en/2023/10/john-chen-retiring-letter-to-blackberry-employees#:~:text=It%20is%20hard%20to%20believe,Company's%20future%20has%20been%20stabilized.

17. BlackBerry Appoints John Giamatteo as CEO [Internet]. blackberry.com. 2023 Dec 11 [Accessed 2025 Jan 29]. Available from: https://www.blackberry.com/us/en/company/newsroom/press-releases/2023/blackberry-appoints-john-giamatteo-as-ceo

BP: Deepwater Horizon's Lingering Shadow

1. BP goes back to petroleum. *Financial Times* [Internet]. 2025 [Accessed 2025 Apr 1]. Available from: https://www.ft.com/content/c7fab097-ecb7-469a-86cd-37fca4ca8e2a

2. BP pivots back to oil and gas after 'misplaced' faith in green energy. *Financial Times* [Internet]. 2025 [Accessed 2025 Apr 1]. Available from: https://www.ft.com/content/8bcf131f-c820-493f-8ea6-6a35440facd3

3. Growing shareholder value: a reset bp. BP.com [Internet]. 2025 Feb 26 [Accessed 2025 Apr 1].
    Available from: https://www.bp.com/en/global/corporate/news-and-insights/press-releases
    /growing-shareholder-value-a-reset-bp.html#07

4. DEEP WATER, The Gulf Oil Disaster and the Future of Offshore Drilling. Report to the President
    National Commission on the BP Deepwater Horizon Oil Spill and Offshore Drilling.
    January 2011.

5. 10 Years Ago: The Deepwater Horizon Oil Spill. National Oceanic and Atmospheric
    Administration [Internet]. [Accessed 2025 Apr 1]. Available from: https://response.restoration.
    noaa.gov/timelines/10-years-ago-deepwater-horizon-oil-spill

6. Hayward – Life Back. YouTube [Internet]. [Accessed 2025 Apr 1]. Available from: https://www.
    youtube.com/watch?v=EZraCNZZ7U8

7. BP Share price. *Financial Times* [Internet]. [Accessed 2025 Apr 2]. Available from:
    https://markets.ft.com/data/equities/tearsheet/charts?s=BP.:LSE

8. President Obama's Oval Office Address on the BP Oil Spill: A Faith in the Future that Sustains
    us as a People [Internet]. [Accessed 2025 Apr 3]. Available from: https://obamawhitehouse.ar
    chives.gov/blog/2010/06/16/president-obamas-oval-office-address-bp-oil-spill-a-faith-future-
    sustains-us-a-peopl#:~:text=But%20make%20no%20mistake%3A%20We,damage%20their%
    20company%20has%20caused

9. Explosion triggered economic, environmental devastation, and a legal battle. National Oceanic
    and Atmospheric Administration [Internet]. [Accessed 2025 Apr 3]. Available from:
    https://www.noaa.gov/explainers/deepwater-horizon-oil-spill-settlements-where-money-
    went#:~:text=Clean%20Water%20Act%2C%20RESTORE%20Act,settlement%2C%20largest%20in
    %20U.S.%20history

10. BP pledges collateral for Gulf of Mexico oil spill trust. [Internet]. 2010 Oct 1 [Accessed 2025
    Apr 3]. Available from: https://www.bp.com/en/global/corporate/news-and-insights/press-
    releases/bp-pledges-collateral-for-gulf-of-mexico-spill.html

11. BP's Deepwater Horizon bill tops $65bn. *The Guardian* [Internet]. [cited 2025 Apr 3]. Available
    from: https://www.theguardian.com/business/2018/jan/16/bps-deepwater-horizon-bill-tops
    -65bn#:~:text=But%20its%20chief%20executive%2C%20Bob,considerably%20by%20rising%
    20oil%20prices

12. Share Price Performance of BP v S&P Global 1200 Index (2009–2025) [Internet]. [Accessed 2025
    Apr 3]. Available from: https://www-capitaliqcom.bournemouth.idm.oclc.org

13. BP Annual Report and Form 20-F 2014, 4–9.

14. Energy (Oil and Gas) Profits Levy. HM revenues and Customs, Gov.UK [Internet]. [cited 2025
    Apr 7]. Available from: https://www.gov.uk/government/publications/changes-to-the-energy-
    oil-and-gas-profits-levy/energy-oil-and-gas-profits-levy#:~:text=As%20oil%20and%20gas%20pri
    ces,to%20the%20levy%20at%20the

15. BP chair Helge Lund to step down. *Financial Times* [Internet]. [Accessed 2025 Apr 7]. Available
    from: https://www.ft.com/content/1bae6dcc-ac08-4007-b5a4-be6b0e24527c

16. BP CEO Tony Hayward to step down and be succeeded by Robert Dudley. BP.com [Internet].
    2010 Jul 27 [Accessed 2025 Apr 8]. Available from: https://www.bp.com/en/global/corporate/
    news-and-insights/press-releases/bp-ceo-tony-hayward-to-step-down-and-be-succeeded-by-
    robert-dudley.html

17. BP Annual Report and Form 20-F, 2010, 10.

18. BP Annual Report and Form 20-F, 2011, 15.

19. BP Annual Report and Form 20-F, 2014, 8.

20. BP chief executive Bob Dudley to retire, to be succeeded by Bernard Looney. BP.com [Internet]. 2019 Oct 4 [Accessed 2025 Apr 9]. Available from: https://www.bp.com/en/global/corporate/news-and-insights/press-releases/bob-dudley-to-retire-to-be-succeeded-by-bernard-looney.html
21. BP Annual Report and Form 20-F, 2019, 4.
22. BP CEO resigns. BP.com [Internet]. 2023 Sep 12 [Accessed 2025 Apr 9]. Available from: https://www.bp.com/en/global/corporate/news-and-insights/press-releases/bp-ceo-resigns.html
23. Murray Auchincloss appointed bp chief executive officer. BP.com [Internet]. 2024 Jan 17 [Accessed 2025 Apr 10]. Available from: https://www.bp.com/en/global/corporate/news-and-insights/press-releases/murray-auchincloss-appointed-bp-chief-executive-officer.html
24. BP's chief aims to more than double market value to $200bn. *Financial Times* [Internet]. [Accessed 2025 Apr 10]. Available from: https://www.ft.com/content/a4c0ea75-a148-4859-aa42-f5d2c58621ba
25. BP profits halve as oil major struggles to turn around business. *Financial Times* [Internet]. [Accessed 2025 Apr 29]. Available from: https://www.ft.com/content/5fc95bea-2849-4994-9b5b-15bdcf750ba4

Wells Fargo & Company: Americas biggest bank, Americas biggest betrayal

1. Enforcement Actions, Wells Fargo Bank, N.A. SEPT 08 2016. Consumer Financial Protection Bureau [Internet]. 2016 Sep 8 [Accessed 2025 Mar 20]. Available from: https://www.consumerfinance.gov/enforcement/actions/wells-fargo-bank-2016/#:~:text=Today%20the%20Consumer%20Financial%20Protection,illegal%20practice%20of%20secretly%20opening
2. $3 Billion Payment Result of Deferred Prosecution Agreement in Criminal Matter, Settlement of Civil Claims under FIRREA and Resolution of SEC Proceedings. U.S. Department of Justice [Internet]. [Accessed 2025 Mar 19]. Available from: https://www.justice.gov/archives/opa/pr/wells-fargo-agrees-pay-3-billion-resolve-criminal-and-civil-investigations-sales-practices#:~:text=Justice.gov-,Wells%20Fargo%20Agrees%20To%20Pay%20%243%20Billion%20To%20Resolve%20Criminal,of%20Millions%20of%20Accounts%20Without
3. CFPB Orders Wells Fargo to Pay $3.7 Billion for Widespread Mismanagement of Auto Loans, Mortgages, and Deposit Accounts. Consumer Financial Protection Bureau [Internet]. [Accessed 2025 Mar 19]. Available from: https://www.consumerfinance.gov/about-us/newsroom/cfpb-orders-wells-fargo-to-pay-37-billion-for-widespread-mismanagement-of-auto-loans-mortgages-and-deposit-accounts/#:~:text=Under%20the%20terms%20of%20the,which%20will%20go%20to%20the
4. Wells Fargo Exhibit A Statement of Facts. U.S. Department of Justice; 2020 Feb 21.
5. How the wheels came off the Wells Fargo stagecoach. Fraud Magazine [Internet]. [Accessed 2025 Mar 19]. Available from: https://www.acfe.com/fraud-magazine/all-issues/issue/article?s=2017-novdec-wells-fargo
6. Wells Fargo Fined $185 Million for Fraudulently Opening Accounts. New York Times [Internet]. 2016 Sep 8 [Accessed 2025 Mar 19]. Available from: https://www.nytimes.com/2016/09/09/business/dealbook/wells-fargo-fined-for-years-of-harm-to-customers.html

7. Wells Fargo & Co, Share price performance. FT.com [Internet]. [Accessed 2025 Mar 19]. Available from: https://markets.ft.com/data/equities/tearsheet/charts?s=WFC:NYQ
8. Share Price Performance of Wells Fargo v S&P Global 1200 Index (2016–2025) [Internet]. [Accessed 2025 Mar 19]. Available from: https://www.capitaliq.spglobal.com/web/client#company/stock?id=100382
9. Wells Fargo & Company. Annual Report 2014. p. 3.
10. Wells Fargo Chief Abruptly Steps Down. New York Times [Internet]. 2016 Oct 13 [Accessed 2025 Mar 25]. Available from: https://www.nytimes.com/2016/10/13/business/dealbook/wells-fargo-ceo.html
11. Wells Fargo Appoints Tim Sloan as CEO and Stephen Sanger as Chairman. Funds Society [Internet]. 2016 Oct 13 [Accessed 2025 Mar 25]. Available from: https://www.fundssociety.com/en/news/appointments/wells-fargo-appoints-tim-sloan-as-ceo-and-stephen-sanger-as-chairman/#:~:text=John%20Stumpf%20steps%20down,Author:%20Gabriela%20Huerta
12. Wells Fargo & Company. Annual Report 2016. p. 5.
13. Wells Fargo & Company. Annual Report 2017. p. 7–10.
14. Wells Fargo Says Its Culture Has Changed. Some Employees Disagree. New York Times [Internet]. 2019 Mar 9 [Accessed 2025 Mar 26].
15. Wells Fargo C.E.O. Timothy Sloan Abruptly Steps Down. New York Times [Internet]. 2019 Mar 28 [Accessed 2025 Mar 26]. Available from: https://www.nytimes.com/2019/03/28/business/wells-fargo-timothy-sloan.html
16. Wells Fargo Names Charles W. Scharf Chief Executive Officer and President [Internet]. 2019 Sep 27 [Accessed 2025 Mar 26]. Available from: https://newsroom.wf.com/English/news-releases/news-release-details/2019/Wells-Fargo-Names-Charles-W.-Scharf-Chief-Executive-Officer-and-President/default.aspx#:~:text=Scharf%20was%20chairman%20and%20CEO,Charlie%20as%20our%20new%20CEO
17. Wells Fargo & Company. Annual Report 2019. p. 10–13.
18. Wells Fargo & Company. Annual Report 2021. p. 5.
19. Wells Fargo & Company. Annual Report 2021. p. 1–2.

Volkswagen AG: Cheat to Compete

1. German economy contracts for second year in succession. Destatis [Internet]. 2025 Jan 15 [Accessed 2025 Mar 4]. Available from: https://www.destatis.de/EN/Press/2025/01/PE25_019_811.html#:~:text=WIESBADEN%20%2D%20According%20to%20first%20calculations,Germany's%202024%20gross%20domestic%20product
2. Volkswagen profit plunges 64% as China sales slide. Financial Times [Internet]. 2024 Oct 27 [Accessed 2025 Mar 4]. Available from: https://www.ft.com/content/b5d916ad-2fda-46cb-838a-070c092861af
3. Volkswagen is in crisis again. Can it be reformed? Financial Times [Internet]. 2024 Oct 26 [Accessed 2025 Mar 4]. Available from: https://www.ft.com/content/a2c7ca01-461c-4dc2-8006-ec1d6b61a066
4. Volkswagen Violations. United States Environmental Protection Agency [Internet]. [Accessed 2025 Mar 4]. Available from: https://www.epa.gov/vw/learn-about-volkswagen-violations#overview

5. VW emissions scandal hits 11m vehicles. BBC News [Internet]. 2015 Sep 22 [Accessed 2025 Mar 4]. Available from: https://www.bbc.co.uk/news/business-34325005

6. Volkswagen CEO Resigns, Saying He's 'Shocked' By Emissions Scandal. NPR News [Internet]. 2015 Sep 23 [Accessed 2025 Mar 5]. Available from: https://www.npr.org/sections/thetwo-way /2015/09/23/442818919/volkswagen-ceo-resigns-saying-he-s-shocked-at-emissions-scandal

7. The Volkswagen Group emissions scandal. UK Parliament [Internet]. 2016 Sep 8 [Accessed 2025 Mar 5]. Available from: https://publications.parliament.uk/pa/cm201617/cmselect/ cmtrans/69/6905.htm

8. Volkswagen to Spend Up to $14.7 Billion to Settle Allegations of Cheating Emissions Tests and Deceiving Customers on 2.0 Liter Diesel Vehicles. U.S. Department of Justice [Internet]. 2016 Jun 28 [Accessed 2025 Mar 5]. Available from: https://www.justice.gov/archives/opa/pr/volks wagen-spend-147-billion-settle-allegations-cheating-emissions-tests-and-deceiving

9. Volkswagen reaches $54 million 'dieselgate' settlement with Italian owners. Reuters [Internet]. 2024 May 15 [Accessed 2025 Mar 5]. Available from: https://www.reuters.com/business/autos-transportation/volkswagen-reaches-54-million-dieselgate-settlement-with-italian-owners-2024-05-15/#:~:text=The%20scandal%20rocked%20the%20automotive,fines%2C%20refits%20and% 20legal%20costs

10. Share Price Performance of VW v S&P Global 1200 Index (2015–2025). Capital IQ [Internet]. [Accessed 2025 Mar 5]. Available from: https://www-capitaliqcom.bournemouth.idm.oclc.org.

11. Volkswagen Group. 2015 Annual Report. p. 5.

12. Matthias Müller appointed CEO of the Volkswagen Group. Porsche Newsroom [Internet]. 2015 Sep 25 [Accessed 2025 Mar 11]. Available from: https://newsroom.porsche.com/en/company/ matthias-mueller-porsche-volkswagen-ceo-11435.html

13. Volkswagen Group. 2015 Annual Report. p. 7.

14. Volkswagen to replace CEO as it tries to make a clean break from its diesel emissions scandal. CNBC [Internet]. 2018 Apr 10 [Accessed 2025 Mar 11]. Available from: https://www.cnbc.com/ 2018/04/10/volkswagen-to-replace-ceo-as-it-tries-to-make-a-clean-break.html

15. Volkswagen Group. 2018 Annual Report. p. 7.

16. Volkswagen Group. 2019 Annual Report. p. 9.

17. Volkswagen top executives charged with market manipulation. BBC News [Internet]. 2019 Sep 25 [Accessed 2025 Mar 11]. Available from: https://www.bbc.co.uk/news/world-europe -49811501#:~:text=Three%20current%20and%20former%20Volkswagen,the%20breadth%20of% 20the%20scandal

18. Trial of former VW boss begins over 'dieselgate' scandal. BBC News [Internet]. 2024 Sep 20 [Accessed 2025 Mar 11]. Available from: https://www.bbc.co.uk/news/articles/cn5r9rgg6yno#:~: text=Indicted%20in%202019%2C%20he%20was,All%20were%20indicted%20in%20Germany

19. Volkswagen CEO apologizes after appearing to reference Nazi slogan. CNN Business [Internet]. 2019 Mar 15 [Accessed 2025 Mar 11]. Available from: https://edition.cnn.com/2019/03/15/busi ness/herbert-diess-volkswagen-ceo-nazi-slogan/index.html

20. Herbert Diess ousted as Volkswagen boss. Financial Times [Internet]. 2022 Jul 22 [Accessed 2025 Mar 11]. Available from: https://www.ft.com/content/f73ee239-8c2a-4344-b042 -2d78c646506b#:~:text=CEO%20forced%20out%20after%20supervisory%20board%20vote,be% 20replaced%20by%20Porsche%20chief%20Oliver%20Blume

21. Volkswagen Group. 2024 Annual Report. p. 5–6.

Acknowledgements

Writing a book is rarely a solitary endeavor, and this one was no exception. I'm genuinely grateful to the many people who have contributed their time, expertise, and unwavering support to bring this book to fruition. First and foremost, I want to thank Martin Reeves, Senior Partner and Chairman of the BCG Henderson Institute, Boston Consulting Group; Robert M. Randall, former Editor of Strategy & Leadership; Satyen Dayal, Managing Director, Edelman (UK); and James Gater, Director, Special Project Partners Ltd for their critical and insightful feedback on an idea that could easily have been dismissed as too left field.

I'd also like to express my gratitude to the entire team at De Gruyter for their hard work and dedication in bringing this book to life. In particular, Matthew Smith, Senior Acquisitions Editor who provided editorial expertise and a great deal of enthusiasm throughout the process and Maximilian Gessl for production advice on how to best present the book. I'm also incredibly grateful to Caroline Oliver, Quynh Nguyen and Sidra Shahid for their research support; your hard work and dedication behind the scenes are truly appreciated.

Finally, and perhaps most importantly, thank you to the readers. I'm incredibly grateful for your interest in my work and I hope that your leap of imagination will have changed your perspective on corporate crisis, culture and performance and that the Corporate Trauma playbook will transform the way you think about your business.

https://doi.org/10.1515/9783111571126-009

About the Author

Prof. Dr. **John Oliver** is a multi-award winning academic-consultant whose research has had a significant impact on both policy and business practice. His work, published in leading international business journals, focuses on the intersection of innovation, crisis management, and strategic organizational transformation. He has a proven track record of generating world-class impact, with his research on the effects of crisis events on innovation and corporate financial performance directly influencing the UK Government's 'Build Back Better: our plan for growth' and the Business, Energy and Industrial Strategy Committee's 'Innovation Strategy'. His research on strategic organizational transformation has influenced UK Communications policy and regulatory decisions, and the public policy debate on internet regulation. This work has also generated financial benefits for several world-class management consultancies, resulting in direct economic impacts such as new jobs and significant financial investments by FTSE 100 firms. Furthermore, the reach and significance of his scenario planning expertise has informed UK Parliament's multi-billion-pound restoration and renewal plan.

Professor Oliver is an advisory board member of the Horizon Scanning & Foresight Committee (Parliamentary Office of Science & Technology) and a member of the Centre of Excellence and Profession in the Enterprise Portfolio Management Office (UK Parliament). He is a former President of the European Media Management Association, a former Visiting Fellow at the University of Oxford, a former Parliamentary Academic Fellow.

https://doi.org/10.1515/9783111571126-010

Index

American International Group Inc. (AIG)
- background 40–41
- corporate crisis 41–44
- corporate financial performance 45–46
- modification in corporate culture 44–45
- transgenerational response over multiple
    corporate generations 47–51
Auchincloss, Murray 83

Balsillie, Jim 64–65, 70, 73
Barclays PLC
- background 52–53
- corporate crisis 53–54
- corporate financial performance 58–59
- modification in corporate culture 56–57
- transgenerational response over multiple
    corporate generations 59–61
Benmosche, Robert H. 48
BlackBerry
- background 63–64
- corporate crisis 64–67
- corporate financial performance 68–70
- modification in corporate culture 67–68
- transgenerational response over multiple
    corporate generations 70–73
Blume, Oliver 105–107
British Petroleum PLC (BP)
- background 74–75
- corporate crisis 75–78
- corporate financial performance 80–81
- modification in corporate culture 78–79
- transgenerational response over multiple
    corporate generations 81–84
Browne, John 75

Cavallo, Daniela 98
Chen, John 71–72, 74
Chief Executive Officer (CEO) 1
- in AIG 47–51
- in Barclays 59–61
- in BlackBerry 70–73
- in British Petroleum PLC (BP) 81–84
- leadership 21–22, 28
- newly appointed 26, 35–37

- role in R&D 34–35
- in Volkswagen AG (VW) 103–106
- in Wells Fargo & Company (WFC) 92–95
chronic corporate underperformance 3, 24–25,
    27, 38
classic turnaround playbook 1, 26, 37, 40, 50–51,
    58, 62–63, 94, 96, 98, 103, 108
communication, strategic 123–125
Consumer Financial Protection Bureau's
    (CFPB) 85–87, 89–92, 96
corporate brand management 4
corporate crisis 16–17, 23, 110
- in AIG 41–44
- in Barclays 53–54
- in BlackBerry 64–67
- in British Petroleum PLC (BP) 75–78
- creates a 'hidden' trauma 27–29
- cultural scars of 30–31
- impact of 4, 16, 23–24, 32, 82, 110
- past crises, future performance 28–29
- in Volkswagen AG (VW) 98–100
- in Wells Fargo & Company (WFC) 86–89
corporate DNA 17, 31–32, 114–115, 119
corporate financial performance 19–21, 45–46
- in AIG 45–46
- in Barclays PLC 58–59
- in BlackBerry 68–70
- in British Petroleum PLC (BP) 80–81
- in Volkswagen AG (VW) 101–103
- in Wells Fargo & Company (WFC) 91–92
Corporate Trauma 2–5
- diagnosing 14–22
- diagnosing cases of 38–107
- playbook 108–125
- understanding 28–29
Corporate Trauma Playbook 108–125
- assessment and diagnosis 109–110
- executing 110–112
cortisol 8–9
COVID-19 pandemic 12, 50, 57–58, 61, 80, 82,
    102
Crackberry. *See* BlackBerry
crisis management and strategic
    communication 4

https://doi.org/10.1515/9783111571126-011